Jane Eyre

A Study Guide

By Francis Gilbert

This edition first published in 2015 by FGI publishing:
www.francisgilbert.co.uk;
fgipublishing.com
Copyright © 2015 Francis Gilbert
FGI Publishing, London UK, sir@francisgilbert.co.uk
British Library Cataloguing-in-Publications Data
A catalogue record for this book is available from the British Library
ISBN-13: 978-1519139795
ISBN-10: 1519139799

Dedication
To my mother

Acknowledgments
First, huge thanks must go to my wife, Erica Wagner, for always supporting me with my writing and teaching. Second, I'm very grateful to all the students and teachers who have helped me write this book.

Also by Francis Gilbert:
I'm A Teacher, Get Me Out Of Here (2004)
Teacher On The Run (2005)
Yob Nation (2006)
Parent Power (2007)
Working The System: How To Get The Very State Education For Your Child (2011)
The Last Day Of Term (2012)
Gilbert's Study Guides on: *Frankenstein, Far From The Madding Crowd, The Hound of the Baskervilles , Pride and Prejudice, The Strange Case of Dr Jekyll and Mr Hyde, The Turn of the Screw, Wuthering Heights* (2013)
Dr Jekyll & Mr Hyde: The Study Guide Edition (2014)
Charlotte Brontë's Jane Eyre: The Study Guide Edition (2015)
Austen's Pride and Prejudice: The Study Guide Edition (2015)
Mary Shelley's Frankenstein: The Study Guide Edition (2015)
Brontë's Wuthering Heights: The Study Guide Edition (2015)

Contents

Part I
Introduction

This study guide takes a different approach from similar books. It does not seek to tell you about the story and characters in a boring, useless fashion, but attempts to show how it is the author's techniques and interests that inform every single facet of this classic novel. Most study guides simply tell you *what* is going on, and tack on bits at the end which tell you *how* the writer created suspense and drama at certain points in the book, informing you a little about *why* the writer might have done this.

This study guide starts with the *how* and the *why*, showing you right from the start *how* and *why* the writer shaped the key elements of the book.

How to use this study guide edition

This study guide is deliberately interactive; it is full of questions, tasks and links to other sources of information. You will learn about the book much more effectively if you have a go at the questions and tasks set, rather than just copying out notes.

Understanding Contexts

In order to fully appreciate a text, you need to appreciate the *contexts* in which it was written – known as its contexts of writing – and the *contexts* in which you read the book, or the contexts of reading.

This is potentially a huge area to explore because 'contexts' essentially means the 'worlds' from which the book has arisen. For the best books, these are many and various. The most obvious starting point is the writer's own life: it is worth thinking about how and why the events in a writer's life might have influenced his or her fiction. However, you do have to be careful not to assume too much. For example, many critics think that the angelic, other-worldly character of Helen Burns in *Jane Eyre* is a representation of Charlotte Brontë's ethereal sister Emily. This may be true, but you must remember that Helen is a character in her own right in the novel – a vital cog in the narrative wheel, a literary construct and not a real person!

As a result, it is particularly fruitful to explore other contexts of writing. We can look at the broader world from which Charlotte Brontë arose (Victorian society and its particular set of values), and consider carefully how, in her writing, she both adopted and rejected the morals of her time. Other contexts might be the influence of the literary world that Brontë inhabited (what other authors were writing at the time), how religion shaped her views, and so on.

Just as important as the contexts of *writing* are the contexts of *reading*: how we read the novel today. Most of us, before we read a classic novel by Charlotte Brontë, have a lot of preconceived ideas about it. Many of us will have seen one or more of the many film versions of the book, and/or been influenced by what we have already heard about the Brontës. Your own personal context is very important too. I think female and male readers may absorb this novel very differently, female readers perhaps falling a little in love with Rochester themselves, and male readers perhaps considering carefully whether they would marry Jane. In order for you to fully consider the contexts of reading rather than my telling you what to think, I have posed open-ended questions that seem to me to be important when considering this issue.

Questions

What do we mean by contexts of writing and reading? Why is it important to consider them when studying *Jane Eyre*, or any work of literature?

Contexts of Writing: Brontë's Life

Some eminent literary critics have argued that Charlotte Brontë was a sexually repressed woman who found that the only outlet for all her passion was through writing.

Surprisingly enough, this argument is not as absurd as it sounds. Brontë really does seem to have had a strong aversion to sex. She refused three offers of marriage, fell in love with a married man whom she knew she could never sleep with, and when she did finally marry the Reverend Arthur Bell Nicholls (near the end of her life when she was 38) it was more out of pity than love. The dangers of having sex are amply illustrated in her most famous novel, *Jane Eyre*: Rochester and Bertha Mason's sexual appetites get them into no end of trouble. It has been argued that the illness of which Brontë died was largely imaginary and that Brontë preferred the idea of death to that of a 'normal' married life.

But before we start saying that Brontë's novels are the product of a sexually repressed, neurotic woman, a few points need to be taken into account. Firstly, any sensible, intelligent woman living in Victorian England should have been scared stiff when contemplating the consequences of having sex: there were no good contraceptives then and a huge number of women died giving birth. Secondly, becoming a married woman – the only way for a 'respectable' woman to have sex – entailed losing what little rights women did have: wives were expected to hand over all their property entirely to their husbands until the Married Women's Property Act of 1870 and 1882. As a married woman Brontë had very little time to write because she was too busy being a dutiful wife.

Trust had to of sucked!

Any careful examination of Brontë's life makes it clear that there were many other factors, other than sexual repression, which motivated her to write. It is often overlooked that the most significant spur for all the Brontë sisters' mature writing was a desperate need for money. In September 1845, when Charlotte discovered some of Emily's poems and tried to get them published, life was very precarious at the Haworth parsonage. The Brontë sisters were the daughters of an ageing cleric from whom they would inherit very little money; their brother Branwell, on whom they had pinned great hopes of making the family fortune, had become an unemployed alcoholic and drug addict; and their other money-making ventures – such as engraving, being governesses and setting up a school at the parsonage – had all failed. As the eldest and most responsible child, Charlotte took it upon herself to promote all their writing as a way of securing an income. The sisters had always been writers: as children they had all invented fantastical imaginary kingdoms and written long and brilliant sagas about them. But Charlotte, a keen reader of fiction, was sharp enough to know that these private fantasies wouldn't sell. So she set about writing a more commercial novel, called *The Professor*, which, although rejected by a notable London publisher, received some favourable feedback. Encouraged, Charlotte wrote *Jane Eyre*, an even more commercial book, combining as it did all the Gothic, fairytale and realist elements which were popular at the time. She also took the wise step of publishing her novels and those of her sisters under genderless pseudonyms so that they wouldn't be dismissed by the male critics as 'women's novels'.

All the great Brontë novels – *Jane Eyre, Emily, Wuthering Heights* and Anne's *Agnes Grey* – appeared within a few months of each other and caused an immense stir. The critics were convinced that they were all written by the same person. In 1848, Charlotte, despite being chronically shy and reluctant to leave her possessive father, travelled with Anne to London and created huge excitement in the press by revealing the true identity of the authors.

But the next two years were horrific for Charlotte: her wayward brother Branwell died of alcoholism, her stoical and introverted sister Emily then died of TB, only to be followed to the grave by Anne, who died of the same disease.

Devastated by these losses, Charlotte persevered and articulated her sense of pain and loneliness in her most mature and difficult novel: *Villette*. This novel draws upon her experiences in Brussels where she had stayed a couple of times during 1842–3 while training to be a teacher. The culture and romance of the city had awakened her mind, while her unspoken obsession with her instructor Monsieur Heger, a married man with children, had nearly broken her spirit. However, like Jane Eyre, Charlotte gained control of her feelings (and unlike her brother Branwell, who had been rejected by a married woman he had declared his love to). The tale of her unrequited feelings was poured into a great deal of her fiction, *Villette* being the most obvious example although fragments of her obsession with

Heger can also be found in *Jane Eyre*.

So we are back to the issue of frustrated love again, but only a very narrow-minded critic would claim that the sole reason for the existence of Brontë's great novels was sexual neurosis.

Selected Reading on Brontë's Life

This biography on the Victorian Web is a good starting point: **http://www.victorianweb.org/authors/bronte/cbronte/brontbio .html**

I thought this YouTube documentary was informative: **https://www.youtube.com/watch?v=QyTeDZZBphI**

Elizabeth C. Gaskell: The Life of Charlotte Brontë, 2 vols (Penguin Classics; first published 1857)

This OCR resource is for teachers, but it contains lots of useful information and can be downloaded as a Word document: **http://www.ocr.org.uk/Images/77062-unit-f661-jane-eyre-lesson-plan-sample.doc**

A controversial book and the first indispensable account of Brontë's life; it remains indispensable today.

Juliet Barker: *The Brontës* (Phoenix; 1994)

A landmark book on the family, brilliantly researched and very detailed.

Lyndall Gordon: *Charlotte Brontë: A Passionate Life* (Vintage; 1995)

A biography which sets out to overturn the conventional view of the suffering heroine. It paints the portrait of a passionate, complex woman and novelist.

Questions

What events, people and ideas in Brontë's life and the wider society may have influenced the writing of *Jane Eyre*? Why is it important to consider her gender and sexuality?

Contexts of Reading

We today read *Jane Eyre* very differently from the way in which the Victorians would have read it. Firstly, our attitudes towards marriage mean that the plot is very definitely situated in the past. Unlike some Victorian novels, *Jane Eyre* could not be updated to a modern day narrative without losing the central dilemma of the book: today Rochester could easily obtain a divorce and would not have hidden his wife in the attic unless he was psychotic – which, for all his passionate ways, he is not! This means we view the novel 'historically', appreciating that it makes sense within the context of its time but that it depicts an era that has mercifully passed in the western world.

Nevertheless it continues to inspire film-makers because, while its central plot device is outmoded, its theme of one woman's search for love and justice is perhaps even more relevant now than it was in the Victorian era. A well-educated, high achieving, feisty woman like Jane Eyre would have been an exception in Victorian England, whereas now these characteristics are perhaps more common. The sort of problems that Jane has to confront – dealing with difficult men, soothing distressed friends, fighting against the prevalent sexism of the culture – are just as pertinent now as they were then.

Moreover, the central dilemma of the book – whether to choose a passionate, difficult partner who promises her an insecure but romantic life, or a sensible, cold partner who offers her a secure but dull life – is very much an issue for both men and women today. The binary opposites that Brontë sets up of insecurity/security, of passion/conformity, of male desire/female desire are all opposites we ourselves try to juggle in our minds.

Our knowledge of the Brontës colours much of what is in the text; before most of us read it, we are aware that the story comes shrouded in the misty Yorkshire moors, cloaked in the tragic story of the dying sisters and their alcoholic brother, and suffused with the mystery of the sisters' brilliant, romantic imaginations. Many of us will have seen one of the many film versions before we read it, with our minds already coloured by Hollywood images of brooding passion and Gothic romance. In this sense, reading the text is like searching for the 'real story', an act of 'unearthing the mystery' of Charlotte Brontë's mind as much as enjoying the narrative.

Remarkably for such an interpreted text, it remains fresh. What leaps out most now is the living, vibrant relationship between Rochester and Jane, which must be the key reason why it remains such an enduringly popular book. How hard many authors have struggled since then to capture such a vivid romance! The power of *Jane Eyre* remains undimmed over 160 years later because of Brontë's characterisations of hero and heroine: their flirtatious, quick-witted banter, their ability to build upon each other's thoughts, their genuine love for each other. At the heart of the novel is the power of their love; in this sense, the novel is timeless.

Useful links

This Wikipedia page contains an exhaustive list of all the film adaptations of the novel:
https://en.wikipedia.org/wiki/Adaptations_of_Jane_Eyre
This IMDB page has reviews of the major film adaptations, including my favourite one with Timothy Dalton; it's an old, creaky adaptation but Dalton is superb as Rochester:
http://www.imdb.com/list/ls003653027/
This webpage is a lively exploration as to why there are so many adaptations:
http://www.slate.com/articles/arts/culturebox/2011/03/up_in _the_eyre.html

Questions

Look at the websites selected here. Why is *Jane Eyre* such a popular novel today? Why have so many films/plays etc. been made of it?

Structure and Theme

There are many ways of summarising this novel because it is so long and contains many sub-plots, all involving the main protagonist, Jane Eyre. However, at the heart of the novel is the notion that it is an edited 'autobiography' – the story of Jane Eyre's life. This is fascinating because an autobiography is, by its very nature, 'non-fictional' and 'truthful', a chronological personal account of a life; but clearly this is a fictional narrative. This element of autobiography enables Brontë to step aside from some of the problems that novelists encounter: e.g. that of generating a story where all the events 'interconnect'. For all its Gothic flights of fancy, there is a realism about *Jane Eyre* – particularly in its descriptions of the squalid conditions at Lowood school, which link it with the socially campaigning novels of Mrs Gaskell.

However, many of the settings and events are basically 'Gothic' in conception: lonely, desolate mansions; terrifying dreams; ghostly laughs in the night; troubled, charismatic, Byronic men; mad women in attics; and improbable coincidences. What makes the novel so enticing is the fact that there is realism in its psychology: Brontë creates a set of believable emotional responses in *Jane Eyre* that hook the reader from the first page. This is because the overwhelming emphasis of the book is its 'autobiographical' impulse: Brontë's repeated insistence on describing in depth Jane Eyre's feelings and thoughts.

So Brontë shapes her narrative around Jane's ongoing struggle to find love and justice in the world. Sometimes these two themes are quite distinct. At the beginning of the book, there is no real sense that the young

Jane is in desperate need of parental love (although this is hinted at); it is more that she is furious with the injustice of her treatment at the hands of the horrid, spoilt child John Reed and his mother, the despicable Mrs Reed. However, the two themes come together when the adult Jane learns of Rochester's bigamy: she has to weigh up her need for just treatment against her craving for Rochester's love. Her desire for justice wins out and she leaves Rochester. Similarly, the themes converge again when St John Rivers proposes to her: he suggests that they live married life as missionaries and bring justice to poor parts of the world, but he offers no real love. This time Jane's need for love triumphs and she rejects him.

We could break down the novel into the following structure:

Opening

Orphan Jane Eyre's childhood and schooling

Her battles for justice and survival against her adopted family

Development of the narrative

Jane's arrival at Thornfield and her growing love for its owner Mr Rochester

Her acceptance of his proposal of marriage

Crisis

Jane's discovery of Rochester's mad wife in the attic, and her refusal, despite her love for him, to become his mistress because it would be morally unacceptable

Her running away and finding sanctuary at Moor House

Climax

Jane's refusal to marry her newly discovered cousin, the curate St John Rivers and become a missionary wife in a loveless but 'just' marriage

Her hearing of Rochester's cry in her head, and her return to Thornfield to learn of the death of Rochester's wife and the destruction of Thornfield itself

Resolution

Her marriage to Rochester

Useful weblinks for the story

The Shmoop summary is very lively and memorable:
http://www.shmoop.com/jane-eyre/summary.html

The Cliff Notes summary is more sedate but worth a look:
http://www.cliffsnotes.com/literature/j/jane-eyre/book-summary
The Spark Notes summary is perfectly fine too:
http://www.sparknotes.com/lit/janeeyre/summary.html
I personally found the Wikipedia summary the best at the time of writing, but sometimes nasty people can change the page and put in deliberate errors:
https://en.wikipedia.org/wiki/Jane_Eyre

Suggested tasks for learning the plot

Read the Shmoop, Cliff Notes and Spark Notes summaries without taking notes, but absorbing the main events of the story, then write either a **visual organizer** of the plot or a summary in your own words.

Or print out one summary of the plot listed above and delete all the inessential information so that you can write a **two paragraph summary of the plot** in your own words.

Or you could have a go at the quizzes on the plot.

SparkNotes has a good quiz here:
http://www.sparknotes.com/lit/janeeyre/quiz.html
CliffNotes has one here:
http://www.cliffsnotes.com/literature/j/jane-eyre/study-help/quiz
GradeSaver has one here:
http://www.gradesaver.com/jane-eyre/study-guide/quiz1
There is the beginning of a Proprofs quiz here:
http://www.proprofs.com/quiz-school/story.php?title=jane-eyre-chapters-14
The Shmoop quiz is the liveliest:
http://www.shmoop.com/jane-eyre/quizzes.html
Or you could answer the comprehension questions I have written at the end of every chapter.

These exercise will really help you get to know the plot properly. Just copying out the plot from study guides will not!

Once you have read the book, ask yourself this question: to what extent is the novel a successful story? What are its exciting moments and why? Are there moments when the story feels less successful? Give reasons for your answers.

Compare one or two filmed versions with the novel; what events/characters/ideas do the film-makers use and what do they leave out, and why?

The Influence of Genre

The Gothic Novel

Having been stung by the rejection of her novel *The Professor*, Brontë very consciously shaped the narrative of *Jane Eyre* around events that might typically be found in Gothic novels. This was a hugely popular genre which had developed in the late eighteenth century. It usually involved a long and complicated narrative of a damsel in distress, trapped in some ghastly castle or mansion, besieged by a sexually rapacious and devious aristocrat, haunted by ghosts and ghouls, chased by innumerable nasties throughout the story, before being rescued by a knight in shining armour, a morally upright man.

Much of what happens at Thornfield, the home of Mr Rochester, follows this pattern.

In many ways, Rochester lives up to the stereotype of the morally suspect, sexually rapacious aristocrat: he attempts to lure Jane falsely into marriage, and then, when he is discovered to have a wife, still persists, claiming that she could live as his mistress. His motivations are undoubtedly sexual. He is presented as a bad-tempered, tempestuous, passionate man who has scant regard for the strict moral codes of the day. Moreover, he inhabits a classic 'Gothic' domain: the mysterious and wonderful Thornfield Hall. It is a place haunted by strange ghostly laughs in the night, unexplained fires, terrifying and inexplicable acts of violence, vast, misty grounds and, perhaps most importantly, forbidden realms: corridors and floors and rooms that are out of bounds. It is, as Jane Eyre herself notes, a true Bluebeard's castle.

This texturing of Thornfield Hall is very deliberate upon Brontë's part, and it is one of the reasons why the novel is so popular now. There is perhaps no better Gothic novel in English. It is marvellously, wonderfully, brilliantly well written because it is so convincing. As we noted before, it is the psychological realism that Brontë brings to the character of Jane Eyre – her feisty, earthy, indomitable reactions to the events and characters of Thornfield – which make the Gothic elements so plausible.

At the heart of this plausibility is Brontë's refusal to allow her main protagonist to be painted as a stereotypical Gothic heroine. Parodied by Jane Austen in her take-off of the Gothic novel *Northanger Abbey*, your average Gothic heroine is forever frightened, forever terrified, always passively running away, avoiding calumny and destruction. Brontë makes a conscious choice for her Gothic heroine to be 'active'. Rather contrary to the stereotype, Jane is forever rescuing the man. This starts with the very first scene in which she encounters Rochester: she helps him up after he has fallen from his horse. Later on, she saves him from being burnt to death in his own bed by his first wife. She even ignores his attempts to persuade her to stay at the house when she learns that her aunt, Mrs Reed, is dying, deciding of her own accord to leave the Gothic realm (a very unusual event in novels of this type).

She is, throughout, the decider of her own destiny. She rejects Rochester's offer of living in sin and leaves; but then she more or less engineers her own proposal of marriage at the end of the novel, happy to be dominant over the 'crippled, blind' Rochester.

Tasks and links

After you have read the novel, devise a **visual organizer** on all the Gothic elements of the book you have found. The Bookrags website has some useful guidance for this here:

http://www.bookrags.com/notes/je/top2.html#gsc.tab=0

This blog is useful too:

http://yikira-englishlit.blogspot.co.uk/2011/05/gothic-forms-in-jane-eyre.html

I found this English Tutor blog the clearest explanation and it contains useful tasks too:

http://englishtutorbournemouth.co.uk/charlotte-bronte-romance-in-jane-eyre/jane-eyre-as-a-gothic-novel-activities-literary-context-language-structure-and-form/

But nothing beats your own investigations!

Answer this question after reading the book: How was Brontë influenced by other writers and genres in the writing of *Jane Eyre*? What elements of the Gothic did she use in the novel and why?

Critical Perspectives: Is *Jane Eyre* a Subversive Novel?

undermine dominant values of a society

Is *Jane Eyre* a subversive novel? One contemporary critic, Mrs Oliphant, was quick to argue that it was. In May of 1855, eight years after the book was published, she wrote in *Blackwood's Magazine*: 'What would happen if social and sexual inferiors asserted that they were the equals of their superiors? ...here is your true revolution.' Mrs Oliphant, along with numerous feminist critics, were convinced that Jane Eyre's demand to be treated as Mr Rochester's equal, despite her lowly social circumstances and her gender, made the novel truly radical.

During the Victorian age, women were considered inferior to men: they were not entitled to vote or study at university and there were very few occupations open to them. Once they were married, all their wealth became their husband's and they had no rights over their children or property. Within this context, Jane's comment, 'but women feel as men feel; ...they suffer from too rigid a restraint', is a very radical one: most people considered that women did not have the sensibilities of men. Likewise Rochester's insistence that Jane was his equal was definitely shocking for contemporary readers: very few 'respectable' husbands of the time ever seriously entertained the notion that their wives were as intelligent as they were.

But there are aspects to the novel which are deeply conservative and seem to endorse an inequality between the sexes and classes. Most troubling is the depiction of Bertha Mason. Rochester informs Jane that it is Bertha's sexual appetites, together with a madness which runs in her family, that has destroyed her sanity. And yet Rochester himself has confessed to a promiscuous past. Whereas Jane's final marriage to Rochester indicates that he is forgiven for his past sins, Bertha's imprisonment shows that she is punished for hers.

The psychoanalytic feminist critics S.M. Gilbert and S. Gubar feel that Bertha represents the truly subversive element in the novel. In their famous book *The Madwoman in the Attic* (London, 1979) they argue that Bertha breaks all the conventions to which women were expected to conform: she is strong, violent and promiscuous, and from a totally different culture from that of everyone else in the book. The ultimate conservatism of the book is underlined by the way in which both Bertha's spirit and culture is either crushed or ignored.

Other critics, such as Hermione Lee, have countered this theory, suggesting that Jane is constantly rebelling against the male-dominated culture of the time and carving her own 'feminist' path. Her initial outcry against John Reed's bullying, her rebuke to Mr Brocklehurst, her abandonment of Rochester, and her rejection of St John Rivers are all indications that she won't be bullied, cajoled or persuaded into accepting a status quo with which she is not content.

But, as Felicia Gordon points out in her excellent book *A Preface to the Brontës* (Longman 1989), for all her rebellious spirit Jane does yearn for a benevolent man to take her under her wing. At the beginning of the novel Jane wishes that her uncle, Mr Reed, were alive so that she wouldn't be subjected to the tyranny of Aunt Reed's rule. At the end, once Rochester is relieved of his mad wife and the question of breaking one of the Lord's commandments has been dismissed, Jane finally does submit to the authority of her husband.

Charlotte Brontë herself was a deeply conservative, God-fearing woman who, despite arguing that women should enjoy more rights, did not want to question the fundamental tenets of the patriarchal society she lived in. However, her genius as a writer forced her to subvert many of the literary conventions of the time: no romantic novels of the period contain such a strong, wilful heroine as Jane, while no Gothic novels depict a character as disturbing as Bertha Mason or a protagonist as complex as Rochester. Even today, very few romantic novels would have the heroine rescuing the hero even once, let alone twice.

The brilliance and complexity of *Jane Eyre* are derived from its being simultaneously a very subversive novel and a deeply conservative one, a novel which radically questions the patriarchal status quo of society and yet ultimately argues for a benevolent male authority.

Selected Reading on *Jane Eyre*

Felicia Gordon: *A Preface to the Brontës* (Longman; 1989)
Part of the Longman Preface series. Of all the A-level guides, this remains the best short introduction to the Brontës that there is: Gordon's concise grasp of the historical and literary context makes this my favourite Preface book of this superb series.

Penny Boumelha *Charlotte Brontë* (Key Women Writers; 1990)
A feminist critique of the book.

Pauline Nestor: *Charlotte Brontë* (Rowman & Littlefield Publishers, Inc.; 1987)
This provides a more traditional critique of the novel and Brontë's work

Useful websites

(A word of warning: while the following websites are useful to look at, please do not copy them blindly. Read them carefully and make your own judgements. Learning these notes off by heart won't help you get a good grade. You will need to think and discuss what you think about the novel for yourself. The highest marks are gained by students who have their **own** views.)

YouTube has a number of videos to help you understand the novel:
CrashCourse Literature's summary is very fast but useful:
https://www.youtube.com/watch?v=Z8tqY8fXoEc
Thug Notes is really funny and actually quite helpful:
https://www.youtube.com/watch?v=lPlN_HIU55U
The Signet Classics' Teachers' Guide to Jane Eyre contains an excellent vocabulary list if you are struggling, good summaries and a useful character list. It's aimed at teachers, but students could easily use it and it's free:
http://www.penguin.com/static/pdf/teachersguides/JaneEyreT G.pdf

The *In Our Time* BBC programme on *Jane Eyre* is excellent and full of useful historical information for a student. It also contains an excellent reading list and links to other websites. It's a great starting point for explorations on the web:
http://www.bbc.co.uk/programmes/b05y11v8

The British Library Resources are great, lots and lots of videos/original manuscripts/critics' views to examine. It's a brilliant place to go after looking at the BBC resources: **http://www.bl.uk/works/jane-eyre**

The BBC History website is good on the Brontë Sisters:
http://www.bbc.co.uk/history/historic_figures/bronte_sisters.s html

The Jane Eyre Society website is worth a look but does not have a wealth of resource. However, the Haworth Parsonage, where the Brontës lived and died, is definitely worth a visit: **https://www.bronte.org.uk/haworth-and-the-brontes/jane-eyre**

This annotated version of the novel is useful because it provides commentaries from the general public and pictures as well. However, a number of chapters have not been annotated:
http://genius.com/albums/Charlotte-bronte/Jane-eyre

The Enthusiast's website to *Jane Eyre* is quirky and not aimed at students particularly (being aimed at fans!) but it contains lots of interesting stuff: **http://eyreguide.awardspace.co.uk/**

The crossref-it.info website is useful on *Jane Eyre*: **http://crossref-it.info/textguide/jane-eyre/9/0**

The Victorian Web contains a wealth of material on the Brontë Sisters: **http://www.victorianweb.org/authors/bronte/cbronte/eyreov.html**

Questions

Once you have read the novel, answer the question I ask in the preceding article: is Jane Eyre a subversive novel still? Do you think it was a subversive novel when it was first published? Give reasons for your answer.

Part II

How to read and study *Jane Eyre*

What follows are selected extracts *Jane Eyre* which are followed by analysis and points for discussion. There are questions on every chapter of the book. This is the best way to get to know the book: have a go at the questions yourself, thinking carefully about them. I have deliberately provided a variety of different question types where I have started with "simple" comprehension questions and then moved onto more analytical and creative questions, which require you to understand more than the plot. Remember if you are uncertain about the plot, you can also refer to the websites listed in the section **'Useful weblinks for the story'**. These websites are good at helping you understand the plot but they won't help you get the higher marks because you really need to think for yourself if you are going to get the top grades.

The Jane Eyre file which I ask you to complete for some chapters should be a "learning journal" which consists of all your thoughts and feelings about her: what has happened to her, what you think of her and what she has done, and any questions you might have about her. You can be creative with this file: draw scenes she might have seen; include spider-diagrams/visual organisers of the people she encounters and the situations she finds herself in; storyboards of the key scenes; copies of articles/literary criticism which you have annotated; creative pieces.

Helpful vocabulary to learn before you start reading

Keeping a vocabulary list is extremely important while reading this book. With the extracts, I have highlighted essential words for learning the spellings/meanings of in **bold**. However, there are some words, I would strongly advise you looking up the meanings of and learning their spellings/meanings *before* reading. These words are the ones highlighted on p. 12-15 of **The Signet Classics' Teachers' Guide to Jane Eyre**. Although this book is aimed at teachers, students should look at it as well. It's free and contains many interesting and valuable notes on the themes, characters and contexts.

There are other more interactive websites which can help too:

This website can signed up to for free and contains flashcards of the difficult vocabulary which you can test yourself on: **https://quizlet.com/792730/jane-eyre-vocab-1-flash-cards/**

This detailed Study Guide, which can be downloaded for free, contains detailed quizzes on the novel, including the vocabulary, starting at p. 45:

http://apliterature7.wikispaces.com/file/view/LP+JaneEyre.p
df

Personally, I find this study guide, along with many others, rather too narrow-minded, but they are good at giving you the 'basics'. You should have a go at the creative and GCSE/A Level style questions if you want to stretch yourself intellectually though in the questions that follow.

Selected Extracts and Questions on Jane Eyre

PREFACE

Questions on the Preface

A useful summary of the Preface can be found here:
http://crossref-it.info/textguide/jane-eyre/9/1018
Summarise, in your own words, five key points that Charlotte Brontë makes in these two prefaces.
Why do you think Charlotte Brontë wrote these prefaces?

CHAPTER I

Extract

There was no possibility of taking a walk that day. We had been wandering, indeed, in the leafless shrubbery *(an area in a garden planted with shrubs/plants)* an hour in the morning; but since dinner (Mrs. Reed, when there was no company, dined early) the cold winter wind had brought with it clouds so sombre *(gloomy)*, and a rain so penetrating, that further out-door exercise was now out of the question.

Analysis: Jane is imprisoned by the bad weather at the beginning of the novel. This is the first "motif" of imprisonment in the book: there are many others and imprisonment forms an important theme throughout the novel. The weather which is "sombre" reflects her mood; this is the first example of pathetic fallacy in the novel (there are many others), where the weather reflects the mood of the main character.

Extract

Folds of scarlet drapery *(cloth hanging in loose folds)* shut in my view to the right hand; to the left were the clear panes of glass, protecting, but not separating me from the drear *(gloomy)* November day. At intervals, while turning over the leaves of my book, I studied the aspect of that winter afternoon. Afar, it offered a pale blank of mist and cloud; near a scene of wet lawn and storm-beat shrub, with ceaseless rain sweeping away wildly before a long and lamentable *(sorrowful)* blast.

Analysis: Note the use of the physical surroundings to convey the mood of the scene and the emotions of the main character, Jane Eyre. The use of <u>pathetic fallacy</u> is important: the weather is "lamentable" or sorrowful thus mirroring Jane's mood.

human feelings to inanimate things

Extract

Accustomed to John Reed's abuse, I never had an idea of replying to it; my care was how to endure the blow which would certainly follow the insult.

"What were you doing behind the curtain?" he asked.

"I was reading."

"Show the book."

I returned to the window and fetched it thence.

"You have no business to take our books; you are a dependent, mama says; you have no money; your father left you none; you ought to beg, and not to live here with gentlemen's children like us, and eat the same meals we do, and wear clothes at our mama's expense. Now, I'll teach you to rummage *(look through)* my bookshelves: for they *are* mine; all the house belongs to me, or will do in a few years. Go and stand by the door, out of the way of the mirror and the windows."

I did so, not at first aware what was his intention; but when I saw him lift and poise the book and stand in act to hurl it, I instinctively started aside with a cry of alarm: not soon enough, however; the volume was flung, it hit me, and I fell, striking my head against the door and cutting it. The cut bled, the pain was sharp: my terror had passed its climax; other feelings succeeded.

"Wicked and cruel boy!" I said. "You are like a murderer—you are like a slave-driver—you are like the Roman emperors!"

Analysis: Brontë introduces here the key theme of the novel: injustice. And she creates in the reader huge sympathy for her character by showing the young Jane Eyre battling against her oppressors without any signs of self-pity.

Discussion point: Where else in the book do we see the writer presenting tyrants in a harsh light?

Questions

1. What does Jane Eyre read and what does this reveal about her character?
2. Why is Jane Eyre sent to the Red Room?
3. What happens overall in this chapter? List five key events.
4. GCSE style question: What makes this opening feel like it is an autobiography? What makes it feel like it is 'made up' or fictional?
5. What parts of the chapter do you not understand? What would help you understand it better?
6. Predict what might happen next.
7. Start a character file on Jane Eyre by listing five to ten key things we have learnt about her personality in this chapter.

Write Jane Eyre's diary for this chapter.

Write a poem called 'The Bully'.

CHAPTER II

Extract

My seat, to which Bessie and the bitter Miss Abbot had left me riveted, was a low ottoman near the marble chimney-piece; the bed rose before me; to my right hand there was the high, dark wardrobe, with subdued, broken reflections varying the gloss of its panels; to my left were the muffled windows; a great looking-glass between them repeated the vacant majesty of the bed and room. I was not quite sure whether they had locked the door; and when I dared move, I got up and went to see. Alas! yes: no jail was ever more secure. Returning, I had to cross before the looking-glass; my fascinated glance involuntarily explored the depth it revealed. All looked colder and darker in that **visionary hollow** than in reality: and the strange little figure there gazing at me, with a white face and arms specking the gloom, and glittering eyes of fear moving where all else was still, had the effect of a real spirit: I thought it like one of the tiny **phantoms**, half fairy, half **imp**, Bessie's evening stories represented as coming out of lone, ferny **dells** in moors, and appearing before the eyes of belated travellers. I returned to my stool.

Analysis: Imprisoned for being disobedient, Jane Eyre is locked in a Red Room and sees herself in the mirror, believing herself to be 'half fairy, half imp', almost a 'real spirit'. Thus Brontë introduces a heavy Gothic element into the novel, but also subverts the Gothic by making the heroine a 'phantom' herself. Later on, Rochester's key way of flirting with Jane will be to call her an 'elfin fairy'.

Discussion point: what do you think of Gothic stories and why?

Extract

A **singular** notion dawned upon me. I doubted not—never doubted—that if Mr. Reed had been alive he would have treated me kindly; and now, as I sat looking at the white bed and overshadowed walls—occasionally also turning a fascinated eye towards the dimly gleaning mirror—I began to recall what I had heard of dead men, troubled in their graves by the violation of their last wishes, revisiting the earth to punish the perjured and avenge the oppressed; and I thought Mr. Reed's spirit, harassed by the wrongs of his sister's child, might quit its abode—whether in the church vault or in the unknown world of the departed—and rise before me in this chamber. I wiped my tears and hushed my sobs, fearful lest any sign of violent grief might waken a **preternatural** voice to comfort me, or **elicit** from the gloom some haloed face, bending over me with strange pity. This idea, consolatory in theory, I felt would be terrible if realised: with all my might I endeavoured to stifle it—I endeavoured to be firm. Shaking my hair from my eyes, I lifted my head and tried to look boldly round the dark room; at this moment a light gleamed on the wall. Was it, I asked myself, a ray from the moon penetrating some aperture in the blind? No; moonlight was still, and this stirred; while I gazed, it glided up to the ceiling and quivered over my head. I can now **conjecture** readily that this streak of light was, in all likelihood, a gleam from a lantern carried by some one across the lawn: but then, prepared as my mind was for horror, shaken as my nerves were by agitation, I thought the swift darting beam was a herald of some coming vision from another world. My heart beat thick, my head grew hot; a sound filled my ears, which I deemed the rushing of wings; something seemed near me; I was oppressed, suffocated: endurance broke down; I rushed to the door and shook the lock in desperate effort.

Analysis: The Gothic atmosphere intensifies when Jane thinks she sees the ghost of the deceased Mr Reed in the room. Brontë sets the tone for the novel in this chapter, always making the reader anxious to question whether the 'Gothic' horrors Jane is encountering are real or supernatural.

Discussion point: Where else in the novel are we uncertain whether an event is real or supernatural? What are the genuine supernatural events of the novel? Or are there any? What do you think the author's attitude is towards the supernatural?

Questions

What scares Jane in the Red Room?
Why does she feel she has been unfairly treated?
GCSE style question: How does Brontë create sympathy for Jane here?
Creative response: continue writing Jane's diary about her experiences.
Update your character file on Jane Eyre.

CHAPTER III

Questions

What does Jane confess to Dr. Lloyd and what do you think of his reaction?
What do the adults in the house accuse Jane of being like and why?
What does Jane learn from Miss Abbot about her family?
Creative response: Write Bessie's diary for this chapter.
GCSE style question: How does Brontë generate suspense during Dr. Lloyd's visit?
Update your file on Jane Eyre.

CHAPTER IV

Extract

"And the Psalms? I hope you like them?"

"No, sir."

"No? oh, shocking! I have a little boy, younger than you, who knows six Psalms by heart: and when you ask him which he would rather have, a gingerbread-nut to eat or a verse of a Psalm to learn, he says: 'Oh! the verse of a Psalm! angels sing Psalms;' says he, 'I wish to be a little angel here below;' he then gets two nuts in recompense for his infant piety."

"Psalms are not interesting," I remarked.

"That proves you have a wicked heart; and you must pray to God to change it: to give you a new and clean one: to take away your heart of stone and give you a heart of flesh."

Analysis: Mr Brocklehurst's visit to the Reeds to prepare Jane for Lowood School leads to Jane's negative judgement of the Psalms and Brocklehurst's response. It sets the tone for the book's continued attack on religious fundamentalism.

Discussion point: Where else in the book do we see Brontë attacking religious fundamentalism in her presentation of the characters? For example, Brontë's presentation of Brocklehurst is highly satirical, suggesting a mockery of his ridiculously rigid thinking about the Bible; how and why does she do this here, and elsewhere in the book? What points arise from her implicit criticisms?

Questions

Who is Mr Brocklehurst? What does he want and what does he think of Jane?

What does Jane accuse Mrs Reed of and why? Why does she think Mrs

Reed is deceitful?

Update your Jane Eyre file for this chapter.

Creative response: write Mrs Reed's diary for this chapter, saying what she thinks of Jane.

GCSE/A Level style question: Although Jane is a child, she is not a victim; how does Brontë manage to convey this in her representation of her?

CHAPTER V

Extract

Ravenous, and now very faint, I devoured a spoonful or two of my portion without thinking of its taste; but the first edge of hunger blunted, I perceived I had got in hand a nauseous mess; burnt porridge is almost as bad as rotten potatoes; famine itself soon sickens over it. The spoons were moved slowly: I saw each girl taste her food and try to swallow it; but in most cases the effort was soon relinquished.

Analysis: Brontë's presentation of Lowood School was based on the author's own experience of attending a school for daughters of clergymen. The most persuasive presentation of the horrors of the school is in the description of the food – its vile tastes and textures. Notice the novel's shift in tone here, moving from the high Gothic melodrama that was generated at Gateshead to the realistic descriptions of a nightmarish girls' school.

Extract

"Can you tell me what the writing on that stone over the door means? What is Lowood Institution?"

"This house where you are come to live."

"And why do they call it Institution? Is it in any way different from other schools?"

"It is partly a charity-school: you and I, and all the rest of us, are charity-children. I suppose you are an orphan: are not either your father or your mother dead?"

Analysis: Here, the young Jane, mystified about why she is attending the school, asks another pupil about it. This leads to a long conversation where aspects of the school's set-up and history are explained to her. Notice how Brontë decides to deliver much of this important information through dialogue, conveying implicitly Jane Eyre's bewilderment at being at the school and providing a convincing child's eye view of the world. Unusually for a writer of her time, she doesn't smother the narrative in adult explanation.

Discussion point: When and why does Brontë use dialogue at this point in the novel?

Questions

What do we learn about Lowood school during Jane's first day?

What makes it such an unpleasant school?

GCSE/A Level style task: Think about Brontë's representation of religion in the book so far. Spider diagram your thoughts.

GCSE/A Level style question: How does she present religious authority in the opening of the novel?

Creative response: write a short story or poem called *The Bad School*.

CHAPTER VI

Questions

What do we learn about Helen Burns here? Why is she punished? How does she respond to her punishment? What are the similarities and differences between Jane and Helen's characters? Devise a chart or visual organiser which compares and contrasts Helen and Jane.

Why do you think Brontë introduces Helen Burns at this point in the novel?

Creative response: either write Helen Burns' diary for this chapter or write a poem about being good and bad, giving it your own title.

CHAPTER VII

Questions

How and why does Mr Brocklehurst "make an example" of Jane?

How does Brontë build suspense during Brocklehurst's visit?

What do we learn about Miss Temple in this chapter?

Creative response: either write Miss Temple's diary for this chapter or write a poem/story called "Humiliation" which is about a student who is "made an example of" like Jane is.

Class or group debate: do you think children need to be punished by adults in order to make sure they behave? Do you think girls should be treated differently from boys in this regard?

Update your file on Jane Eyre, writing summary notes about what has happened at Lowood.

CHAPTER VIII

Questions

What does Helen mean when she says Jane is "too impulsive, too vehement"? Do you think she's right?

Why does Miss Scatcherd put the word "Slattern" on Helen's forehead? What is Jane's reaction? How is Brontë playing with the reader's emotions here?

What favour does Miss Temple do for Jane?

Who are the protagonists and antagonists in the novel so far? Draw up a chart of them, showing how they are similar and different, and then write an essay where you compare and contrast the main characters in the book.

CHAPTER IX

Extract

"But where are you going to, Helen? Can you see? Do you know?"

"I believe; I have faith: I am going to God."

"Where is God? What is God?"

"My Maker and yours, who will never destroy what He created. I rely **implicitly on His power**, and confide wholly in His goodness: I count the hours till that eventful one arrives which shall restore me to Him, reveal Him to me."

"You are sure, then, Helen, that there is such a place as heaven, and that our souls can get to it when we die?"

"I am sure there is a future state; I believe God is good; I can resign my immortal part to Him without any misgiving. God is my father; God is my friend: I love Him; I believe He loves me."

"And shall I see you again, Helen, when I die?"

"You will come to the same region of happiness: be received by the same mighty, universal Parent, no doubt, dear Jane."

Analysis: The death of the saintly Helen Burns, who together with the aptly named Miss Temple has guided Jane through the horrors of Lowood, marks the end of this section of the book. Once again, the theme of justice is implicitly raised. Underlying much of the dialogue that Jane has with the dying Helen is the question: would a fair God do this? Helen's answer, like Brontë's sister Emily's, is emphatic: there is a better place. But notice the ambivalence in Jane's tone. It is one of the best of the many Victorian death scenes in literature because of its relative lack of sentimentality, which makes it all the more moving.

Discussion point: If you are re-reading the novel, how does the death of Helen contrast with the death of Mrs Reed, which happens later on in the novel? What point do you think Brontë is trying to make about the way death reveals people's true natures?

Questions

How does the outbreak of illness affect Lowood? How does the natural world contrast with the situation at Lowood?

How does Brontë build suspense in this chapter?

How and why does Helen Burns die? What do you think of Helen Burn's attitude towards her death?

What does "Resurgam" mean and why is it significant do you think?

Think about the symbolism in the novel so far, particularly in the names of people and places: the Red Room, Lowood, Gateshead, Jane Eyre, Helen Burns, Miss Temple, Mr Brocklehurst, Scatcherd. What do these names suggest in terms of feelings, the elements, and states of mind?

CHAPTER X

Questions

Why is Jane upset when Miss Temple gets married? What does she now wish for at Lowood and why?

What advert does Jane reply to and why? What is the response?

What does Jane learn from Bessie about Mrs Reed, her children and Mr Eyre's visit to Gateshead?

Update your Jane Eyre file: what do we learn here about how she has changed since she was a child? How do her talents and achievements compare with the Reed children's accomplishments?

What do you think is going to happen next? Predict what might happen in the next phase of Jane's life.

A Level style question: what techniques does Brontë use to reveal the development and maturing of Jane's character in this chapter?

CHAPTER XI

Extract

"She is Mr. Rochester's ward; he commissioned me to find a governess for her. He intended to have her brought up in ---shire, I believe. Here she comes, with her 'bonne,' as she calls her nurse." The enigma then was explained: this affable and kind little widow was no great dame; but a dependant like myself. I did not like her the worse for that; on the contrary, I felt better pleased than ever. The equality between her and me was real; not the mere result of **condescension** on her part: so much the better—my position was all the freer.

Analysis: Brontë builds up a considerable degree of suspense before she introduces Rochester, making him a mysterious and absent landlord at first. And she deliberately makes Mrs Fairfax as bland as possible.

Discussion point: Why do you think Brontë takes so long before introducing Rochester, her main male protagonist, into the novel?

Questions

What is Jane worried about before she gets to Thornfield Hall? How are her fears allayed?

What is Mrs Fairfax like?

Who does Jane initially think is the owner of Thornfield Hall and who does she learn is the real owner? What does she learn about the owner?

What is Thornfield Hall like? Draw and label a picture, using the descriptions of the house if you want.

What laugh does Jane hear which troubles her? What explanation does Mrs Fairfax give for the laugh?

GCSE style question: How does Brontë create suspense in this chapter?

Update your file on Jane Eyre, providing notes on her first impressions of Mrs Fairfax, Adele and Grace Poole.

A Level style question: What literary devices does Brontë use to make her descriptions of the Hall intriguing and effective?

Creative response: write a descriptive account of a spooky place, using some of the techniques deployed by Brontë in her descriptions if you can.

CHAPTER XII

Extract

Something of daylight still lingered, and the moon was **waxing** bright: I could see him plainly. His figure was **enveloped** in a riding cloak, fur collared and steel clasped; its details were not apparent, but I traced the general points of middle height and considerable breadth of chest. He had a dark face, with stern features and a heavy brow; his eyes and gathered eyebrows looked **ireful** and **thwarted** just now; he was past youth, but had not reached middle-age; perhaps he might be thirty-five. I felt no fear of him, and but little shyness. Had he been a handsome, heroic-looking young gentleman, I should not have dared to stand thus questioning him against his will, and offering my services unasked. I had hardly ever seen a handsome youth; never in my life spoken to one. I had a **theoretical reverence** and **homage** for beauty, **elegance, gallantry**, fascination; but had I met those qualities **incarnate** in masculine shape, I should have known instinctively that they neither had nor could have sympathy with anything in me, and should have shunned them as one would fire, lightning, or anything else that is bright but **antipathetic**.

Analysis: Brontë presents Rochester as 'stern', 'ireful' and 'thwarted' from the very start of her introduction to him. In many ways, the ensuing narrative between Jane and Rochester will be both a dramatisation and explanation of these very qualities, with 'thwarted' being the operative word. He is, above all, presented as a discontented, accident-prone character. This episode sets up the pattern for most of their significant interactions: a discovery and a rescue on Jane's part, and some sort of tortured, flirtatious, elliptical explanation on Rochester's part, which never quite satisfies Jane or the reader; each time a significant event happens we tend to find that Jane 'rescues' Rochester – namely from a fire, from a mad wife, from insupportable immorality, from desolate loneliness – and discovers a little more about him in the process. However, when she discovers something about him, the story is never fully unearthed. We are always asking questions about the situation – even at the very end of the novel. Their major interactions are focused around these discoveries.

Discussion point: What is attractive and mysterious about this presentation of Rochester?

Extract

"I am the governess."

"Ah, the governess!" he repeated; "deuce take me, if I had not forgotten! The governess!" and again my raiment underwent scrutiny. In two minutes he rose from the stile: his face expressed pain when he tried to move.

"I cannot commission you to fetch help," he said; "but you may help me a little yourself, if you will be so kind."

"Yes, sir."

"You have not an umbrella that I can use as a stick?"

"No."

"Try to get hold of my horse's bridle and lead him to me: you are not afraid?"

I should have been afraid to touch a horse when alone, but when told to do it, I was disposed to obey. I put down my muff on the stile, and went up to the tall steed; I **endeavoured** to catch the **bridle**, but it was a spirited thing, and would not let me come near its head; I made effort on effort, though in vain: meantime, I was **mortally** afraid of its trampling fore-feet. The traveller waited and watched for some time, and at last he laughed.

Analysis: Throughout the novel, Jane seems to be overcoming her fears; she does so here with the horse and it provokes Rochester's laughter.

Discussion point: What is endearing about the presentation of Jane in this passage? How is Brontë managing to generate the sensation of the two characters becoming emotionally tied together even at this early stage?

Questions

What is life at Thornfield Hall like before the arrival of Mr Rochester? What is Adèle like as a student?

How does Jane help the man on the horse? Who is the man on the horse? What is his age and what does he look like? What kind of personality does he seem to have? Why do you think we only learn his identity at the end of the chapter?

GCSE style question: How does Brontë make the first meeting between Jane and Mr Rochester unusual and striking? Look carefully at her use of description, action and dialogue.

Creative response: write a prediction of what might happen next.

Update your file on Jane Eyre, noting down her reactions to the arrival of Rochester.

CHAPTER XIII

Mrs. Fairfax had dropped her knitting, and, with raised eyebrows, seemed wondering what sort of talk this was.

"Well," resumed Mr. Rochester, "if you disown parents, you must have some sort of kinsfolk: uncles and aunts?"

"No, none that I ever saw."

"And your home?"

"I have none."

"Where do your brothers and sisters live?"

"I have no brothers or sisters."

"Who recommended you to come here?"

"I advertised, and Mrs. Fairfax answered my advertisement."

Analysis: It is worth noting this first example of the flirtation between Jane and Rochester in full because it exemplifies the authorial techniques that Brontë employs to generate such a powerful connection between Rochester and Jane. After all, it is their relationship which ultimately elevates the novel above Gothic melodrama. Brontë presents Rochester as an utterly confident conversationalist who, like a deft swordsman, makes faints and asides that often bewilder his social inferiors; but here Jane rises to his challenges. His initial statements about her teaching are flattering, but then he follows them with the discontented 'Humph!' and the barking order, 'Come to the fire!' Then he pursues Jane with questions about her past, showing real interest, but peppers his rigorous interrogation with flirtatious comments about her bewitching him. Notice how Jane relishes the chance to adopt his metaphors, while trying to negate his claim that she is a fairy: 'The men in green all forsook England a hundred years ago.'

Discussion point: How does Brontë generate such a sense of sexual tension between Jane and Rochester?

Extract

"What about?"

"Family troubles, for one thing."

"But he has no family."

"Not now, but he has had—or, at least, relatives. He lost his elder brother a few years since."

"His *elder* brother?"

"Yes. The present Mr. Rochester has not been very long in possession of the property; only about nine years."

"Nine years is a tolerable time. Was he so very fond of his brother as to be still inconsolable for his loss?"

"Why, no—perhaps not. I believe there were some misunderstandings between them. Mr. Rowland Rochester was not quite just to Mr. Edward; and perhaps he prejudiced his father against him. The old gentleman was fond of money, and anxious to keep the family estate together. He did not like to diminish the property by division, and yet he was anxious that Mr. Edward should have wealth, too, to keep up the consequence of the name; and, soon after he was of age, some steps were taken that were not quite fair, and made a great deal of mischief. Old Mr. Rochester and Mr. Rowland combined to bring Mr. Edward into what he considered a painful position, for the sake of making his fortune: what the precise nature of that position was I never clearly knew, but his spirit could not brook what he had to suffer in it. He is not very forgiving: he broke with his family, and now for many years he has led an unsettled kind of life. I don't think he has ever been resident at Thornfield for a fortnight together, since the death of his brother without a will left him master of the estate; and, indeed, no wonder he shuns the old place."

Analysis: It is from this small section that Jean Rhys was inspired to *Wide Sargasso Sea* which tells the tale of Rochester's first wife. It is an important part of the novel but is often overlooked.

Discussion point: what do you think Mrs Fairfax's account of Rochester's early life and family tell us about him and the society he lived in?

Questions

How and why does Thornfield Hall change with the arrival of Rochester? Why is Jane Eyre not embarrassed by Rochester's rude and "irate" manner?

What do we learn from Rochester about Jane Eyre's teaching skills?

Why is Rochester impressed that Jane is still alive and well after being at Lowood school? What does this tell us about his knowledge of the area?

What does Rochester accuse Jane of doing to his horse?

What pictures of Jane's impressed Rochester and why?

What does Jane think of Rochester at this point?

Why has Rochester not been very long in possession of Thornfield Hall? Why does Mrs Fairfax think he is troubled?

Add to your Jane Eyre file, noting down her reactions and thoughts to Rochester.

GCSE/A Level style question: how does Brontë make Rochester a mysterious and intriguing figure in this chapter?

CHAPTER XIV

Extract

"Ah! By my word! there is something singular about you," said he: "you have the air of a little **nonnette**; quaint, quiet, grave, and simple, as you sit with your hands before you, and your eyes generally bent on the carpet (except, by-the-bye, when they are directed piercingly to my face; as just now, for instance); and when one asks you a question, or makes a remark to which you are obliged to reply, you rap out a round rejoinder, which, if not blunt, is at least brusque. What do you mean by it?"

> Analysis: The protagonists of the novel are famously plain (unlike the movie versions!). Rochester's perceptions of Jane are interesting because in contrast to all others they are not negative, but full of a sense of attraction. Interestingly, the reader is uncertain about whether Rochester is right: we have perceived Jane as almost the opposite of a fairy. For the reader, she is earthy, passionate, committed.

> Discussion point: What is the effect of making the main protagonists plain, perhaps even ugly? How do you see them in your eyes?

Questions

Why do you think Rochester asks Jane to say whether he is handsome or not? How and why does her reply surprise him and worry Jane once she has said it?

What does Rochester confess to Jane in this chapter? Why is she confused?

How does Brontë maintain interest and narrative drive in the dialogue between Jane and Rochester? How does she create a deepening sense of mystery?

CHAPTER XV

Extract

Mr. Rochester did, on a future occasion, explain it. It was one afternoon, when he chanced to meet me and Adèle in the grounds: and while she played with Pilot and her **shuttlecock**, he asked me to walk up and down a long beech avenue within sight of her.

He then said that she was the daughter of a French opera-dancer, Céline Varens, towards whom he had once cherished what he called a *"grande passion."*

> Analysis: Here, Rochester's Byronic qualities are evident: it is clear that he was the lover of a French opera-dancer. Jane's lack of moral judgement upon him is worth noting. While Brontë is happy to reveal that Rochester was something of a 'rake' before the cataclysmic revelation of his bigamy, she also reveals Jane's response as being tolerant; thus she paves the way for the suspense of the chapters in which Jane must decide whether or not to be Rochester's mistress. The neutral language in which she describes Rochester's behaviour with Céline Varens gives the reader the sense that Jane might be 'open minded' enough to accept the status of a mistress. Thus suspense is generated by the shifting attitudes of Jane's moral conscience.

> Discussion point: What were the attitudes towards mistresses in Brontë's day?

Extract

This was a **demoniac laugh**—low, suppressed, and deep—uttered, as it seemed, at the very keyhole of my chamber door. The head of my bed was near the door, and I thought at first the goblin-laugher stood at my bedside—or rather, crouched by my pillow: but I rose, looked round, and could see nothing; while, as I still gazed, the unnatural sound was reiterated: and I knew it came from behind the panels. My first impulse was to rise and fasten the bolt; my next, again to cry out, "Who is there?"

Something gurgled and moaned. Ere long, steps retreated up the gallery towards the third-storey staircase: a door had lately been made to shut in that staircase; I heard it open and close, and all was still.

"Was that Grace Poole? and is she possessed with a devil?" thought I. Impossible now to remain longer by myself: I must go to Mrs. Fairfax. I hurried on my frock and a shawl; I withdrew the bolt and opened the door with a trembling hand. There was a candle burning just outside, and on the matting in the gallery. I was surprised at this circumstance: but still more was I amazed to perceive the air quite dim, as if filled with smoke; and, while looking to the right hand and left, to find whence these **blue wreaths** issued, I became further aware of a strong smell of burning.

Something creaked: it was a door ajar; and that door was Mr. Rochester's, and the smoke rushed in a cloud from thence. I thought no more of Mrs. Fairfax; I thought no more of Grace Poole, or the laugh: in an instant, I was within the chamber. Tongues of flame darted round the bed: the curtains were on fire. In the midst of blaze and vapour, Mr. Rochester lay stretched motionless, in deep sleep.

"Wake! wake!" I cried. I shook him, but he only murmured and turned: the smoke had stupefied him. Not a moment could be lost: the very sheets were kindling, I rushed to his basin and **ewer**; fortunately, one was wide and the other deep, and both were filled with water. I heaved them up, **deluged** the bed and its occupant, flew back to my own room, brought my own water-jug, baptized the couch afresh, and, by God's aid, succeeded in **extinguishing** the flames which were **devouring** it.

The hiss of the **quenched element**, the **breakage of a pitcher** which I flung from my hand when I had emptied it, and, above all, the splash of the shower-bath I had **liberally bestowed**, roused Mr. Rochester at last. Though it was now dark, I knew he was awake; because I heard him **fulminating strange anathemas** at finding himself lying in a pool of water.

"Is there a flood?" he cried.

"No, sir," I answered; "but there has been a fire: get up, do; you are quenched now; I will fetch you a candle."

"In the name of all the **elves in Christendom**, is that Jane Eyre?" he demanded. "What have you done with me, witch, sorceress? Who is in the room besides you? Have you plotted to drown me?"

"I will fetch you a candle, sir; and, in Heaven's name, get up. Somebody has plotted something: you cannot too soon find out who and what it is."

"There! I am up now; but at your peril you fetch a candle yet: wait two minutes till I get into some dry garments, if any dry there be—yes, here is my dressing-gown. Now run!"

I did run; I brought the candle which still remained in the gallery. He took it from my hand, held it up, and surveyed the bed, all blackened and scorched, the sheets drenched, the carpet round swimming in water.

"What is it? and who did it?" he asked. I briefly related to him what had transpired: the strange laugh I had heard in the gallery: the step ascending to the third storey; the smoke,—the smell of fire which had conducted me to his room; in what state I had found matters there, and how I had deluged him with all the water I could lay hands on.

Analysis: It is Jane's hearing of the laughter which saves Rochester. Laughter plays a very important role in the novel, to generate a sense of both menace and love: Rochester is always laughing at Jane. Many critics have also commented upon the elemental aspects of the novel: Brontë's use of fire, water, air and earth. Here, it is Jane's hearing of the laughter in the *air* which leads to her to the *fire*; she stops it with *water* and thus prevents Rochester being buried in the *earth*. Jane's surname 'Eyre' also invokes the element of 'air', being its homophone. It serves to give the narrative a mythical, elemental undercurrent which gives additional emotional significance to the events.

Discussion point: Why and how does Brontë make use of the four elements in the rest of the novel?

Extract

He re-entered, pale and very gloomy. "I have found it all out," said he, setting his candle down on the washstand; "it is as I thought."

"How, sir?"

He made no reply, but stood with his arms folded, looking on the ground. At the end of a few minutes he inquired in rather a peculiar tone—

"I forget whether you said you saw anything when you opened your chamber door."

"No, sir, only the candlestick on the ground."

"But you heard an odd laugh? You have heard that laugh before, I should think, or something like it?"

"Yes, sir: there is a woman who sews here, called Grace Poole,—she laughs in that way. She is a singular person."

"Just so. Grace Poole—you have guessed it. She is, as you say, singular— very. Well, I shall reflect on the subject. Meantime, I am glad that you are the only person, besides myself, acquainted with the precise details of to-night's incident. You are no talking fool: say nothing about it. I will account for this state of affairs" (pointing to the bed): "and now return to your own room. I shall do very well on the sofa in the library for the rest of the night. It is near four:—in two hours the servants will be up."

"Good-night, then, sir," said I, departing.

He seemed surprised—very inconsistently so, as he had just told me to go.

"What!" he exclaimed, "are you quitting me already, and in that way?"

"You said I might go, sir."

"But not without taking leave; not without a word or two of acknowledgment and good-will: not, in short, in that brief, dry fashion. Why, you have saved my life!—snatched me from a horrible and **excruciating** death! and you walk past me as if we were mutual strangers! At least shake hands."

Analysis: Just as important as the rescue itself is this aftermath which is really the trigger for Jane to begin feeling love for Rochester. It is a surprising and affecting scene: we are not quite sure what Rochester will ask of her – we are not quite sure about him at all – but we are gratified by his gratitude towards her.

Discussion point: How does Brontë use the incident of this rescue to generate more suspense and anticipation, both here and in the rest of the novel?

Questions

What happened between Adèle's mother, Céline Varens, and Rochester? Why does he confess this to Jane, do you think?

What "glare" does Rochester give when he looks up at the battlements of Thornfield? What is his mood at this point? Why do you think he looks this way?

Why does Rochester not believe Adèle is his daughter despite that her mother says she is?

Why does Rochester think that Jane may want to leave her post as governess now she has learnt about what happened between Rochester and Céline?

What sound does Jane hear in the night? How does she save Rochester's life? What is strange about his reaction to the fire? Why do you think he wants Jane to say nothing about the incident?

GCSE/A Level style question: How does Brontë create a Gothic atmosphere in the last part of this chapter, from the time Jane wakes up in the night to the end of the chapter?

Why are the elements significant and symbolic in this novel: fire, water, air and earth?

Update your Jane Eyre file, including the details about Rochester's French mistress and the fire.

CHAPTER XVI

Questions

What surprises Jane about Grace Poole's manner and why?

According to Mrs Fairfax, where has Rochester visited? What does Jane about Blanche Ingram from Mrs Fairfax? Why does this information disturb her?

How does Brontë maintain the mystery and romance about Rochester in this chapter?

It's time again to examine the connotations and symbolism of the names in the book. What are the connotations of these names: Pilot, Gytrash, Edward Rochester, Grace Poole, Mrs Fairfax, Blanche Ingram, Céline and Adèle Varens.

CHAPTER XVII

Extract

"Who would not be the **Rizzio of so divine a Mary**?"

"A fig for Rizzio!" cried she, tossing her head with all its curls, as she moved to the piano. "It is my opinion the **fiddler David must have been an insipid sort of fellow**; I like **black Bothwell** better: to my mind a man is nothing without a spice of the devil in him; and history may say what it will of **James Hepburn**, but I have a notion, he was just the sort of wild, fierce, bandit hero whom I could have consented to gift with my hand."

"Gentlemen, you hear! Now which of you most resembles Bothwell?" cried Mr. Rochester.

"I should say the preference lies with you," responded Colonel Dent.

"On my honour, I am much obliged to you," was the reply.

Miss Ingram, who had now seated herself with proud grace at the piano, spreading out her snowy robes in queenly amplitude, commenced a brilliant prelude; talking meantime. She appeared to be on her high horse to-night; both her words and her air seemed intended to excite not only the admiration, but the amazement of her auditors: she was evidently bent on striking them as something very dashing and daring indeed.

"Oh, I am so sick of the young men of the present day!" exclaimed she, rattling away at the instrument. "Poor, puny things, not fit to stir a step beyond papa's park gates: nor to go even so far without mama's permission and guardianship! Creatures so absorbed in care about their pretty faces, and their white hands, and their small feet; as if a man had anything to do with beauty! As if loveliness were not the special prerogative of woman— her **legitimate appanage and heritage**! I grant an ugly *woman* is a blot on the fair face of creation; but as to the *gentlemen*, let them be **solicitous** to possess only strength and valour: let their motto be:—Hunt, shoot, and fight: the rest is not worth a **fillip**. Such should be my device, were I a man."

"Whenever I marry," she continued after a pause which none interrupted, "I am resolved my husband shall not be a rival, but a foil to me. I will suffer no competitor near the throne; I shall exact an **undivided homage**: his devotions shall not be shared between me and the shape he sees in his mirror. Mr. Rochester, now sing, and I will play for you."

Analysis: The introduction of Blanche Ingram enables Brontë to draw a marked contrast between Jane and a lady of society. It is the only time when real social satire is introduced: the portrait of Blanche is satirical, mocking her pretensions and her vapid life.

Discussion point: Does the introduction of the Blanche Ingram subplot slow down the novel, stopping us from getting to the real action, the real mystery? Or is it a vital part of the story?

Questions

What preparations are made at the house for the party?

Why do you think Rochester insists that Jane attends the party?

How is the English class system portrayed in this chapter? Think about the representation of Blanche Ingram as a symbol of the English upper classes and Jane as emblematic of someone with very low social status. Blanche's business is to find a rich, upper-class husband, while Jane, as an orphan, is expected to work.

Why is Blanche Ingram so insulting about governesses?

Why does Jane leave the party?

Why does Rochester follow her?

How successful is Brontë in making Blanche an "antagonist" – a character in a story who opposes the protagonist or represents a serious threat to the protagonist.

Creative response: write a story called 'The Party' in the first person in which there is a character like Jane who attends a party where everyone makes them feel like an outsider. Make the descriptions and dialogue lively: you can set the story in the present day if you like.

CHAPTER XVIII

Questions

What charade does Rochester act out with Blanche?

How do Rochester and Blanche act towards each other after the charades?

What does Jane think of Blanche and her relationship with Rochester?

How and why has Jane "learnt to love" Rochester?

Why is Jane not in "jealousy and despair" about Blanche?

Where is Mr Mason from? What is he like as a person? What does he say his relationship to Rochester is? Describe his appearance and manner.

What kind of "vagabond" turns up at the house? Why are the guests excited by her? Who goes to see her first and what is her mood when she returns?

What will happen next when Jane goes to see the vagabond, do you think?

Creative response: write a story called 'The Stranger' in which a stranger comes to stay at your house who knows one of your parents, but you can't work out the relationship. How does your mum/dad really know them?

CHAPTER XIX

Questions

What three things does the gypsy tell Jane she is and how does the gypsy justify these points?

What does Jane tell the gypsy her ambition is?

What does the gypsy tell Jane about her character?

Who is the gypsy really? What is Jane's reaction to this news?

What is Rochester's reaction when he learns that Mr Mason has come to visit? How does Brontë create suspense here?

GCSE-style question: How does Brontë create an atmosphere of both comedy and menace in this chapter?

Update your Jane Eyre file for this section of the novel, making notes on how she has come to learn to love Rochester, her thoughts on Blanche and the gypsy fortune teller.

Creative response: write a poem called 'The Fortune Teller'.

CHAPTER XX

Extract

"Here, Jane!" he said; and I walked round to the other side of a large bed, which with its drawn curtains concealed a considerable portion of the chamber. An easy-chair was near the bed-head: a man sat in it, dressed with the exception of his coat; he was still; his head leant back; his eyes were closed. Mr. Rochester held the candle over him; I recognised in his pale and seemingly lifeless face—the stranger, Mason: I saw too that his linen on one side, and one arm, was almost soaked in blood.

"Hold the candle," said Mr. Rochester, and I took it: he fetched a basin of water from the washstand: "Hold that," said he. I obeyed. He took the sponge, dipped it in, and moistened the corpse-like face; he asked for my smelling-bottle, and applied it to the nostrils. Mr. Mason shortly unclosed his eyes; he groaned. Mr. Rochester opened the shirt of the wounded man, whose arm and shoulder were bandaged: he sponged away blood, trickling fast down.

"Is there immediate danger?" murmured Mr. Mason.

Analysis: Brontë brilliantly paces her narrative. Having introduced the ghastly laugh, described the fire in Rochester's bed, she now ups the tension with a violent attack on the poor Mr Mason, a mysterious person himself. Notice again how Rochester has to rely on Jane to help him help Mason. For once, Rochester is helping someone, but not a woman: a man.

Discussion point: Why is Brontë's description of the wounded Mason so effective? What verbs and adjectives does she use to make it so alarming? What is effective about her use of dialogue?

Questions

What noise does Jane hear in the middle of the night? How many times does she hear it and what does it sound like?

What does Rochester tell the guests to do?

How does Jane help Rochester?

What has happened to Mr Mason, do you think? Summarise in a couple of sentences what he and Rochester talk about. Who do you think wanted to "suck" Mason's blood?

After the long, difficult night, Rochester and Jane walk in the beautiful garden. What do they talk about? What question does Rochester ask Jane and what is her reply? Who does it look like he is intending to marry?

What do you think will happen next?

GCSE-style question: How does Brontë create a Gothic mood of drama and mystery in this chapter? How does she use description and dialogue to create this mood?

Creative response: write a poem or story called 'The Attack'.

CHAPTER XXI

Extract

I obeyed her directions. "Read the letter," she said.

It was short, and thus conceived:—

"Madam,—Will you have the goodness to send me the address of my niece, Jane Eyre, and to tell me how she is? It is my intention to write shortly and desire her to come to me at Madeira. Providence has blessed my endeavours to secure a competency; and as I am unmarried and childless, I wish to adopt her during my life, and bequeath her at my death whatever I may have to leave.—I am, Madam, &c., &c.,

"JOHN EYRE, Madeira."

It was dated three years back.

"Why did I never hear of this?" I asked.

"Because I disliked you too **fixedly** and thoroughly ever to lend a hand in lifting you to prosperity. I could not forget your conduct to me, Jane—the fury with which you once turned on me; the tone in which you declared you abhorred me the worst of anybody in the world; the unchildlike look and voice with which you affirmed that the very thought of me made you sick, and asserted that I had treated you with miserable cruelty.

Analysis: The way in which the death scene of Mrs Reed interrupts the dramatic goings on at Thornfield Hall is almost frustrating, but Brontë wishes us to see that Jane has matured: she does not **rebuke** the old, embittered woman in the same way that she did as a child.

Discussion point: To what extent does the modern reader feel Jane has matured? Clearly Brontë wants to show that Jane has acquired the important Victorian quality of **stoicism**, but today this is a less fashionable quality and perhaps we sympathise more with the rebellious child who speaks her mind rather than **represses** it?

Questions

What are the three things that make life so mysterious, according to Jane Eyre? Look at the first paragraph of this chapter to find the answer.

Who has married Bessie?

What happened to John Reed and why? When Mrs Reed heard of this news, what happened to her?

Why does Jane feel she needs to leave Thornfield Hall for two weeks? What does Rochester say when he hears this news? What discussion do Rochester and Jane have over money?

Why does Jane say that she probably should find a new job soon? How does Rochester react to this suggestion?

How have the Reed family changed since Jane last saw them?

What does Jane learn from the dying Mrs Reed about her long lost uncle in Madeira? What did Mrs Reed tell him and why? What is Jane's reaction?

A Level/GCSE style question: How does Brontë show the development of Jane Eyre's character in this chapter? Do you think this chapter conveys any moral messages in its representation of the Reed family?

CHAPTER XXII

Questions

Why is Jane surprised by her feelings when she returns to Thornfield Hall?

What else is surprising considering that there is going to be a marriage soon?

GCSE/A Level style question: How does Thornfield Hall contrast with Gateshead? Write an extended piece whi

CHAPTER XXIII

Extract

"Gratitude!" he **ejaculated**; and added wildly—"Jane accept me quickly. Say, Edward—give me my name—Edward—I will marry you."

"Are you in earnest? Do you truly love me? Do you sincerely wish me to be your wife?"

"I do; and if an oath is necessary to satisfy you, I swear it."

"Then, sir, I will marry you."

"Edward—my little wife!"

"Dear Edward!"

"Come to me—come to me entirely now," said he; and added, in his deepest tone, speaking in my ear as his cheek was laid on mine, "Make my happiness—I will make yours."

"God pardon me!" he subjoined ere long; "and man meddle not with me: I have her, and will hold her."

"There is no one to meddle, sir. I have no kindred to interfere."

Analysis: Huge suspense surrounds the marriage proposal because it has been so drawn out: the interruptions of Blanche Ingram, the attack on Mason, and the visit to Gateshead to Mrs Reed have all meant that it has been delayed. When it comes it is Jane's passionate declaration of love that prompts it, because she is so distraught at the thought of Rochester marrying Blanche. Then, when he first proposes, she believes she is being mocked. Unusually for the time, he offers her a share of his property, indicating that while this will be no union of financial equals he wishes to give her some independence.

Discussion point: Look at Jane's final acceptance of Rochester. How effective is it? Is the sudden introduction of his first name affecting or rather ridiculous? What does it signify?

Questions

Why does Jane burst into tears?

Why does Rochester suddenly confess that he has no intention of marrying Miss Ingram?

Why does Jane doubt Rochester when he asks to marry her?

What happens to the horse-chestnut in the night? Why is this event symbolic?

When you've finished the novel, can you work out the significance of Rochester pointing out a West Indian insect to Jane?

This chapter is generally acknowledged as marking the first climactic event of the novel. How does Brontë make the proposal so memorable?

CHAPTER XXIV

Questions

Why does Jane not want to be showered with gifts or taken on a tour of Europe as Rochester would like to do with her?

What is Mrs Fairfax worried about?

What do Rochester and Jane argue over at Milcote?

Why does Jane keep Rochester at a distance during the courtship, do you think?

GCSE/A Level style question: How does Brontë foreshadow the trouble to come in this chapter?

CHAPTER XXV

Questions

What does Jane tell Rochester happened in her room the previous night? Who has she seen there? What is the significance of the tearing of the veil, do you think?

What has Jane dreamt about?

How does Brontë make this chapter Gothic in tone and approach? How she create real suspense and horror here?

Update your Jane Eyre file, adding notes on the marriage proposal, Jane's worries and the "Vampyre" in her room.

CHAPTER XXVI

Extract

Mr. Rochester continued, hardily and recklessly: "Bigamy is an ugly word!—I meant, however, to be a bigamist; but fate has out-manoeuvred me, or Providence has checked me,—perhaps the last. I am little better than a devil at this moment; and, as my pastor there would tell me, deserve no doubt the sternest judgments of God, even to the **quenchless** fire and deathless worm. Gentlemen, my plan is broken up:—what this lawyer and his client say is true: I have been married, and the woman to whom I was married lives! You say you never heard of a Mrs. Rochester at the house up yonder, Wood; but I daresay you have many a time inclined your ear to gossip about the mysterious lunatic kept there under watch and ward. Some have whispered to you that she is my **bastard** half-sister: some, my cast-off mistress. I now inform you that she is my wife, whom I married fifteen years ago,—Bertha Mason by name; sister of this resolute personage, who is now, with his quivering limbs and white cheeks, showing you what a stout heart men may bear.

Analysis: In one of the most dramatic wedding scenes in all English literature, Mr Rochester's plan to marry is foiled by Richard Mason, the brother of Bertha, who returns to Thornfield with a lawyer to prove that Rochester is indeed married. The scene is notable for Rochester's response and the minimal emotion evinced by Jane at this point. Rochester's lack of remorse, his passionate confession, and the way he shows Bertha to the rest of the world all suggest that Brontë wants to present someone who is almost relieved to confess, but is not sorry that he tried to marry Jane. He is clearly contemptuous of the edicts of the church, seeing them only as a means to marry Jane. This implicit atheism was shocking for the time, but also understandable within the context of Romantic poets such as Percy Bysshe Shelley who married but were atheists.

Discussion point: To what extent do you think Brontë presents Rochester as a villain who has been unmasked at the wedding?

Extract

"Keep out of the way," said Mr. Rochester, thrusting her aside: "she has no knife now, I suppose, and I'm on my guard."

"One never knows what she has, sir: she is so cunning: it is not in mortal discretion to fathom her craft."

"We had better leave her," whispered Mason.

"Go to the devil!" was his brother-in-law's recommendation.

"'Ware!" cried Grace. The three gentlemen retreated simultaneously. Mr. Rochester flung me behind him: the lunatic sprang and grappled his throat **viciously**, and laid her teeth to his cheek: they struggled. She was a big woman, in stature almost equalling her husband, and corpulent besides: she showed virile force in the contest—more than once she almost **throttled** him, athletic as he was. He could have settled her with a well-planted blow; but he would not strike: he would only wrestle. At last he mastered her arms; Grace Poole gave him a cord, and he **pinioned** them behind her: with more rope, which was at hand, he bound her to a chair. The operation was performed amidst the fiercest yells and the most **convulsive** plunges. Mr. Rochester then turned to the spectators: he looked at them with a smile both acrid and desolate.

"That is *my wife*," said he. "Such is the sole **conjugal** embrace I am ever to know—such are the endearments which are to **solace** my leisure hours! And *this* is what I wished to have" (laying his hand on my shoulder): "this young girl, who stands so grave and quiet at the mouth of hell, looking collectedly at the gambols of a demon, I wanted her just as a change after that fierce ragout. Wood and Briggs, look at the difference! Compare these clear eyes with the red balls yonder—this face with that mask—this form with that bulk; then judge me, priest of the gospel and man of the law, and remember with what judgment ye judge ye shall be judged! Off with you now. I must shut up my prize."

Analysis: Many modern critics have noted Brontë's presentation of Bertha as an animal – as someone who is not human but a 'hyena', only worthy of the pronoun 'it', a maniac with shaggy hair. However, there is a virulent, aggressive sensuality in the description which suggests the sexual allure that Rochester responded to in marrying her; she is 'corpulent' and strong and tall like Rochester, his physical equal. Notice too that he refrains from hitting her but 'wrestles', and that this is redolent of the sexual act. Indeed, Rochester comments sarcastically that it is the only conjugal embrace he gets. The description of her as 'purple' and 'bloated' suggests her alien nature, her otherness.

Discussion point: To what extent do you think the description of Bertha is essentially racist? From the descriptions of Rochester and Bertha together, what do you think their relationship was and is like?

Questions

Who stops the marriage and why? Who is this man accompanied by?

What does Rochester admit to? Where does he take the party and what do they see there?

What prompted Mr Mason to intervene?

How does make a this such an exciting and dramatic chapter?

Update your Jane Eyre file, adding in what her thoughts and feelings are about the marriage being stopped.

Creative response: write a description of a person who people think is a monster/vampire etc, but actually is not. Or write a story called 'The Wedding That Went Wrong'.

CHAPTER XXVII

Extract

"You know I am a scoundrel, Jane?" ere long he inquired **wistfully** — wondering, I suppose, at my continued silence and tameness, the result rather of weakness than of will.

"Yes, sir."

Analysis: We learn about Jane's moral judgement of Rochester through dialogue rather than the expression of her thoughts. He himself provides the word 'scoundrel', which is interesting. A 'scoundrel' was a man driven by his passions – his sexual passions in particular; he used his intellect as a means to pursue sexual satisfaction.

Discussion point: Do you think Rochester is presented as a scoundrel or as a victim of his own passions? Or is he presented as both simultaneously?

Extract

"Of course: I told you you should. I pass over the madness about parting from me. You mean you must become a part of me. As to the new existence, it is all right: you shall yet be my wife: I am not married. You shall be Mrs. Rochester—both virtually and nominally. I shall keep only to you so long as you and I live. You shall go to a place I have in the south of France: a whitewashed villa on the shores of the Mediterranean. There you shall live a happy, and guarded, and most innocent life. Never fear that I wish to lure you into error—to make you my mistress. Why did you shake your head? Jane, you must be reasonable, or in truth I shall again become frantic."

His voice and hand quivered: his large nostrils dilated; his eye blazed: still I dared to speak.

"Sir, your wife is living: that is a fact acknowledged this morning by yourself. If I lived with you as you desire, I should then be your mistress: to say otherwise is **sophistical** —is false."

Analysis: Jane is quick to see that Rochester's arguments in favour of keeping her are false in their logic. She sees that his offer would involve her living in sin. Here, reading the novel within the context of Helen Burns's religious beliefs makes sense: Jane, for all her hatred of religious fundamentalism and hypocrisy, is profoundly religious. The marriage vow is inviolate and cannot be broken. This is probably true of Charlotte Brontë herself, who, while in Belgium, struggled with her own passions for a married man but decided that she could not become his mistress. Implicit here perhaps is an attack upon the rigid institution of marriage, although it is not something to which Brontë **explicitly** draws the reader's attention. The impossibility of divorce seems harsh to the modern reader.

Discussion point: Would this be a believable moral dilemma for a modern novel? If not, why not? In what way have attitudes towards marriage have changed since the Victorian era?

Extract

"Mr. Rochester, I no more assign this fate to you than I grasp at it for myself. We were born to strive and endure—you as well as I: do so. You will forget me before I forget you."

"You make me a liar by such language: you sully my honour. I declared I could not change: you tell me to my face I shall change soon. And what a distortion in your judgment, what a perversity in your ideas, is proved by your conduct! Is it better to drive a fellow-creature to despair than to transgress a mere human law, no man being injured by the breach? for you have neither relatives nor acquaintances whom you need fear to offend by living with me?"

Analysis: Rochester here begins to articulate what cannot be fully expressed: that the marriage laws forbidding divorce were unreasonable, even if made by God. The idea has become more powerful with time.

Discussion point:What role does time play in the novel?

Questions

What does Jane's conscience tell her she must do?
What does Rochester tell Jane about Bertha Mason? What does Rochester mean by looking for 'the Antipodes of the Creole'? What were the problems Rochester found with Bertha Mason?
Why does Jane refuse to become his mistress?
How and why does Jane leave Thornfield Hall?
Look back over the novel and draw a concept map of how the elements are represented in the novel: earth, air, fire, water. Think about the symbolism of these things, for example when Jane pours water over Rochester's burning bed, the fire in this chapter, Jane's love of bird who fly in the air, the "earthiness" of Bertha Mason, her lust for sex etc.
How does Brontë make this a suspenseful and surprising chapter? How does she deepen the characterisations of Rochester and Jane?

CHAPTER XXVIII

Questions

What happens to Jane which makes life very difficult for her? Why is she forced to beg?
Why does the servant at the St. John Rivers' household refuse to help Jane? Who comes to Jane's rescue and why?
Why does she say her name is 'Jane Elliot', do you think?
Why does Jane suffer because of her gender? What do you think the book says about the position of women in Victorian society, both in this chapter and in the novel as a whole?
How does Brontë generate "pathos" (feelings of pity) for Jane in this chapter?
Creative response: write a poem or story called 'Homeless'.
Add to your Jane Eyre file, noting down what has happened to her in this chapter and why she leaves Rochester.

CHAPTER XXIX

Extract

Mr. St. John—sitting as still as one of the dusty pictures on the walls, keeping his eyes fixed on the page he perused, and his lips mutely sealed—was easy enough to examine. Had he been a statue instead of a man, he could not have been easier. He was young—perhaps from twenty-eight to thirty—tall, slender; his face riveted the eye; it was like a Greek face, very pure in outline: quite a straight, classic nose; quite an **Athenian** mouth and chin.

Analysis: Jane's fleeing from Thornfield and her eventual surfacing at Moor House, the home of St John Rivers, marks the end of the 'crisis' section of the book. Now begins a long build-up to the eventual climax: her rediscovery of Rochester and her marriage to him. It is Brontë's thematic control which sustains the interest here. At the back of the reader's mind is the question about what will happen to Rochester and Jane, but this is secondary to our interest in how Jane will now fare having rejected a tempting but sinful offer of living with her loved one. The laws of God have triumphed over her own passions. Now Brontë explores these themes further in her presentation of St John Rivers: he is presented as the complete antithesis of Rochester. The imagery employed is striking: he is like a Greek statue, with a straight nose. Younger than Rochester, St John Rivers is someone whose reason always overrules his passion: his love for Rosamund Oliver is overruled by his belief that she is unsuitable, that she arouses too much passion in him, and that Jane is a much better and more suitable candidate... precisely because he does not love her.

Discussion point: What do you think of the Rivers family? How is the household similar and different to Thornfield?

Questions

How does Hannah insult Jane? What is Jane's response?

What are the two names for the house they are staying in? Why do these names have symbolic meanings?

What does Jane learn has happened to the St. Rivers' family?

Why is Jane embarrassed about whether she is a spinster or not?

What story does Jane tell St. Rivers about why she came to Marsh End? How is she caught out regarding her surname? What reply does she give?

What is St. Rivers like as a person? What are his sisters like? What do they do?

Write Jane Eyre's diary about her impressions of the St. Rivers' household.

Or write a story/poem called: "The Stranger Who Came To Stay."

CHAPTER XXX

Questions

What does Jane like about the St. Rivers' home?
How is St. John Rivers similar and different to his sisters?
Why does Jane think that St. John Rivers has not found peace? What are his religious views?
Why do the sisters have to leave Moor House?
What job does St. John Rivers offer Jane? Why does he feel the job will be degrading for her? What is her reply?
What does St. John tell Jane about how his family lost all their money?
How does Brontë create a sense of mystery here?

CHAPTER XXXI

Questions

Who provides Jane with her cottage?
What does Jane find difficult about her teaching job at first?
What question does Jane ask herself about her life choices?
What does St. John Rivers worry Jane might be feeling when he visits her?
Why was St. John Rivers wanting to die a year ago? What stopped his misery?
What is Miss Rosamund Oliver like physically and psychologically?
What does Jane think St. John Rivers feels for Miss Oliver despite what he wants to feel?
Write St. John Rivers' diary for this chapter, discussing his feelings for Jane and Rosamund. Or write a story called 'The person I didn't want to love'.

CHAPTER XXXII

Questions

How and why does Jane's relationship with her pupils change?
What nightmares does Jane have and why?
What does St. John Rivers say he should do after he gives Jane a book of poetry and looks at her portrait of Rosamund? What does he admit to Jane about his feelings towards Rosamund? Why, though, is he conflicted about his feelings for her? What kind of missionary's wife does he feel Rosamund

would make and why?

How does Brontë create suspense at the end of this chapter? What do you think will happen next?

CHAPTER XXXIII

Questions

How does Brontë create suspense at the beginning of the chapter when St. John Rivers enters?

What "tale" does St. John Rivers tell Jane and why?

When St. John Rivers calls Rochester a "bad man" how does Jane react and why?

How did St. John Rivers discover that she is Jane Eyre?

How and why has Jane Eyre become an "heiress"? What does she decide to do with the money?

What do you think of the "co-incidence" at this point in the novel? Do you think it works as a "plot device"? Many stories – fairytales, Shakespeare's plays, Victorian novels – use similar co-incidences at the end of their stories. Why do you think Brontë might have inserted this co-incidence at this point? There is no wrong or right answer.

CHAPTER XXXIV

Questions

What is the mood of the sisters at Christmas? How do they feel about the changes Jane has made to the house?

How does St. John Rivers mood contrast with the women?

What language does Jane learn with St. John Rivers and why?

What proposal does St. John Rivers make to Jane? What is her response?

How does Brontë build up a picture of St. John Rivers' character in this chapter?

How does Brontë create suspense in this chapter?

Write a poem called 'The Proposal' or write a diary entry from one of the sister's viewpoints.

CHAPTER XXXV

Questions

Why does St. John Rivers continue to urge Jane to marry him? What is her response?

Why does Diana think Jane would be a fool to go to India with her brother?

Why does Jane feel she should marry St. John Rivers? What "voice" stops her from marrying him?

Why and how does Brontë make the end of the chapter so thrilling, mysterious and suspenseful?

Write a character study of St. John Rivers, thinking about how he is similar and different to the other religious figures in the novel: Helen Burns and Mr Brocklehurst. What narrative role does he play in the story? How is he an ambivalent figure?

Write a poem/story called 'The Voice' about a voice that calls to someone, speaking to them either from the grave or a long distance.

Update your Jane Eyre file, talking about her time at Moor House, her feelings towards the St. Rivers' family, her discovery of her fortune, and the choice offered to her by St. John Rivers to go and be a missionary in India.

CHAPTER XXXVI

Extract

"Then Mr. Rochester was at home when the fire broke out?"

"Yes, indeed was he; and he went up to the attics when all was burning above and below, and got the servants out of their beds and helped them down himself, and went back to get his mad wife out of her cell. And then they called out to him that she was on the roof, where she was standing, waving her arms, above the battlements, and shouting out till they could hear her a mile off: I saw her and heard her with my own eyes. She was a big woman, and had long black hair: we could see it streaming against the flames as she stood. I witnessed, and several more witnessed, Mr. Rochester ascend through the sky-light on to the roof; we heard him call 'Bertha!' We saw him approach her; and then, ma'am, she yelled and gave a spring, and the next minute she lay smashed on the pavement."

"Dead?"

"Dead! Ay, dead as the stones on which her brains and blood were scattered."

"Good God!"

Analysis: It is fascinating to see how the energy returns to Brontë's writing when describing the ghastly events at Thornfield. It is a welcome relief after the muted domestic drama at Moor House. Once Jane hears in her head Rochester's voice calling her back to him, we realise that we have returned to the realm of the Gothic – to a different world, where passion and madness prevail. As with many key parts of the novel, the death of Bertha is conveyed in dialogue – Rochester's butler explains it after Jane has walked around the shattered, burnt-out husk of Thornfield. We learn that Rochester, as a result of trying to save Bertha unsuccessfully from dying, is now a blind cripple. There is something profoundly symbolic and moral about his fate: he is punished by God for his sins. And now he is free to be loved again.

Discussion point: To what extent do you think Brontë presents Rochester as a character who deserves his fate?

Questions

What doubts does Jane have about hearing Rochester's voice? What does St. John's note tell her to do?

Why does she go to Thornfield?

Why is she shocked when she sees Thornfield?

What does she learn from the host of the Rochester Arms had happened during the fire at Thornfield Hall?

Where has Rochester gone to live and why?

What is the effect of the story about Rochester upon the reader?

How does Brontë make the story very Gothic in atmosphere at this point?

Write Jane Eyre's diary for this chapter, discussing what she has seen and learned, as well as exploring her feelings.

CHAPTER XXXVII

Extract

"You cannot now wonder," continued my master, "that when you rose upon me so unexpectedly last night, I had difficulty in believing you any other than a mere voice and vision, something that would melt to silence and annihilation, as the midnight whisper and mountain echo had melted before. Now, I thank God! I know it to be otherwise. Yes, I thank God!"

He put me off his knee, rose, and reverently lifting his hat from his brow, and bending his sightless eyes to the earth, he stood in mute devotion. Only the last words of the worship were audible.

"I thank my Maker, that, in the midst of judgment, he has remembered mercy. I humbly entreat my Redeemer to give me strength to lead henceforth a purer life than I have done hitherto!"

Then he stretched his hand out to be led. I took that dear hand, held it a moment to my lips, then let it pass round my shoulder: being so much lower of stature than he, I served both for his prop and guide. We entered the wood, and wended homeward.

Analysis: At the end of the novel, Rochester is presented as someone who has discovered the enlightened ways of God but whose passionate nature remains intact. In this way, Brontë subtly brings her moral purposes to a close: the passionate have had their natures tempered and punished by fire, both literal and metaphorical.

Discussion point: What significance does fire have in the novel? How is it connected with passion?

Questions

How does Jane first see Rochester again? How is he similar but different from before?

When Rochester realises Jane is in the room with him what does he think she is?

How does Brontë make this meeting both romantic and passionate?

Why does Rochester ask Jane repeatedly to marry him in this chapter?

What does Rochester confess he did a few nights before in desperation? Why is this rather spooky? Why does Jane not tell him that she heard his voice?

Write Rochester's diary for this chapter.

Write a poem called 'The Return'.

CHAPTER XXXVIII— CONCLUSION

Reader, I married him. A quiet wedding we had: he and I, the parson and clerk, were alone present. When we got back from church, I went into the kitchen of the manor-house, where Mary was cooking the dinner and John cleaning the knives, and I said—

"Mary, I have been married to Mr. Rochester this morning."

> **Analysis:** The famous conclusion of the novel is notable for its sentence structure, which contains an incipient feminism. Brontë did not write 'he married me' but 'I married him', indicating that it is now Jane who is in charge of her own destiny. It has taken her to be in possession of her own fortune, for her fiancé to be blinded and crippled, but, at the very end of the novel, she now has genuine power over Rochester.

> **Discussion point:** To what extent do you think this is a feminist ending to the novel?

Questions

What kind of marriage do Jane and Rochester have?

How do the following respond to the news of Jane's marriage: Mary, Adèle, St. John Rivers and his sisters.

How does Jane help Adèle?

What happens to Rochester's eyesight? What child is born and why is the restoration of Rochester's sight important at this point?

What happened to St. John Rivers?

Update your Jane Eyre file including all the details of her seeing Rochester again and her marriage.

How successful is the ending of the novel in your view?

Speaking and Listening Exercises on the novel

Work in a group and devise a **chatshow** based on the novel. Make sure that you have an interviewer (chat-show host) who questions the main characters in the novel about their thoughts and feelings regarding what has happened to them. You can be quite "free" with who you invite on the show. For example, Bertha Mason could come on as a "ghost" (!) to explain her views, or you could invite Charlotte Brontë on the show to talk about why she created the characters in the novel. The aim is that students need to show that they understand the storyline and characters by talking in role about the events in the novel.

You could put Rochester on **trial** for his treatment of Bertha Mason. Set things up so that you have a prosecuting lawyer who is accusing Rochester of crimes against his wife, including manslaughter for the death of Bertha. Have a defence lawyer who argues that there is evidence Rochester was compelled to do the things he did. Call witnesses for the prosecution and defence who are characters from the novel or the author, or literacy critics; remember many feminist and post-colonial critics claim that Rochester is a representative of the evils of patriarchy and colonialism (see section on Literary Critics). Use the trial to explore different views on the novel. Then possibly write it up as a script or review what you have learnt from doing it.

Put the main characters in **therapy**. Have them visit a therapist to discuss their problems with the therapist. You could do this so that they go into therapy at various stages during the novel, i.e. John Reed could talk to a therapist when he is an adult, Jane/Rochester/St. John Rivers could talk to the therapist after major events in the novel. Plan it out first and devise a mini-drama using the therapist sessions to reveal your knowledge of the characters' motivations and the story. Write a review of what you have learnt from doing this afterwards.

Work in a group and devise a **radio drama** of the major parts of the novel. Different groups could work on different sections of the book; e.g. Jane's time at Gateshead, Lowood, Thornfield, Moor House, Ferndean. Use the text where appropriate, cutting it down drastically and write some dialogue or using Brontë's dialogue where appropriate. Make the drama short and punchy. This exercise will help you get to know the text in much more depth: the editing of the novel will help you summarise key points.

The Literary Critics on *Jane Eyre*

Traditional critics

Some critics, some still living but most from previous generations, take what might be called a "traditional" approach to the novel, i.e. analyse the novel using the typical tools of the literary critics, examining the effectiveness of its storyline, its characters, its themes, its imagery and use of language. More traditional critics have sought to argue that *Jane Eyre* is a "timeless" novel in that its themes and narrative are relevant to people from all eras and places. They have pointed out that the plot of the novel is exciting, compelling the reader to keep turning the pages to find out what happens next. They have tended to treat the characters in the novel very much like "real people", investigating their motivations in depth, talking about how the characters are very similar to people you might meet in real life: Jane is the poor girl searching for meaning and love, the Reeds are typical bullies and tyrants, Brocklehurst is indicative of fundamentalist Christians and Rochester is a conflicted man, torn between duty and love.

Furthermore, a number of traditional critics have drawn attention to the Christian symbolism of the novel; Jane Eyre is rather like the Pilgrim in John Bunyan's **Pilgrim's Progress (1678)** in which Jane makes a spiritual journey towards the "Celestial City" or heaven in a similar way to the Pilgrim in Bunyan's allegory. In order to do so, she has to pass through various places, all of which have symbolic meanings. There is Gateshead, which suggests the "gate" of hell, with its bullying, neglectful atmosphere. She then descends to "Lowood" which is a "low wood", an even more miserable place than Gateshead, a further descent into hell: there is the chronic religious hypocrisy of Brocklehurst, illness, the death of Helen Burns, and even worse material deprivations there. She progresses on to the fairy-tale realm of "Thornfield" which is like the place where her thorn-encircled "sleeping beauty" (Rochester) lies, it is a liberating place for her, but also a place of darkness, disappointment and betrayal. From there she moves on to "Moor House" or "Marsh End" which connote the boggy moors, a place of confusion but also a location where she can gain her "moorings". Finally, she finds her "true self", her heaven, her man, in "Ferndean", a name which is evocative of a beautiful wood and a real contrast to the "thorniness" of Thornfield. Other traditional critics like Q.D. Leavis (introduction to **Penguin edition, 1966**) have argued that the novel has a very satisfying structure, with its representation of the development and maturing of Jane. She argues like many critics have done that the novel's brilliance lies in the way it is a "deeply felt" novel, full of emotions which resonate with the reader.

Radical critics

Jane Eyre has always divided critics: is it a conservative novel or a radical one? More recently, radical critics have sought to reassess the novel. These are critics who look at literary texts in ways that either are radically different or politically radical, or both. Marxist critics of the novel such as Terry Eagleton in **The English Novel from Dickens to Lawrence (1975)** have pointed out the novel reveals a society which is in the process of huge social change. The fact that the lower-class Jane is able to marry an upper-class person like Rochester shows that the social barriers that stopped different social classes from inter-marrying were breaking down. Marxist critics aim to explore texts in the ways in which they reveal the class system, which they, being Marxist, feel is unfair. Thus *Jane Eyre* reveals the unfairness of the class system: it shows that while the smallest misdemeanours of the lower classes are punished very severely, an upper class person like Rochester is able to get away with imprisoning his wife, attempted bigamy and behavior which would not be tolerated amongst the lower-classes.

Feminist critics like Sandra Gilbert and Susan Gubar in **The Madwoman in the Attic: The Woman Writer and the Nineteenth-Century Literary Imagination (1979)** explore the theme of injustice even further with regards to the treatment of women. They argue that Bertha Mason, the imprisoned wife, is a neglected figure in the novel, but coded within the novel, for all its condemnation of Bertha for her wildness, her sexual appetites, is an awareness that woman are treated unfairly compared with men. This, they argue, was probably not Brontë's view, but is a view that can be drawn out from a careful reading of the novel because the very things that Rochester is allowed to get away with (wildness, sexual appetite, immorality), Bertha appears to have been punished for in a much more extreme way than Rochester. Jean Rhys explores this idea in **Wide Sargasso Sea (1966)**, telling Bertha Mason's story and revealing how Bertha was originally called Antoinette and was effectively sold off to Rochester in a deal carried out by her brother, Richard Mason. Rhys reveals how Rochester could not cope with Antoinette's sexuality and, as a result of his desire to claim her inheritance and his disgust at her 'lust', he renames her Bertha Mason and imprisons her. He is portrayed as a terrible patriarchal villain. Rhys explores the novel from a "colonial" perspective, describing the Caribbean island where Antoinette grew up in poetic detail and showing how the British colonised the island, cruelly suppressing the indigenous natives even after slavery was abolished. Many other recent critics, sometimes called post-colonial critics, have explored the colonial aspects of the novel as well such as Gayatri Spivak in **Three Women's Texts and a Critique of Imperialism**. Spivak, in very theoretical language, explores how the novel reveals colonial attitudes towards colonised people; Bertha is a "colonised" subject and is effectively a metaphor for what happened to the colonies under British rule; they were imprisoned by British codes and values, devalued, dehumanised and destroyed by the crushing hand of imperial rule. Thus Bertha becomes a symbol of colonial oppression.

Useful links:

There is an excellent video and discussion about the position of women in *Jane Eyre* on the British Library's website here: **http://www.bl.uk/romantics-and-victorians/articles/jane-eyre-and-the-19th-century-woman**

There is another excellent resource about *Jane Eyre* and fairytales on the British Library's website here: **http://www.bl.uk/romantics-and-victorians/articles/jane-eyre-fairytale-and-realism**

Task

What do you think of the different perspectives of the novel?

How to Write a Top Grade Essay on *Jane Eyre*

In order to write a good essay about *Jane Eyre*, you need to understand it. You will need to know what the difficult vocabulary means and be aware of how the text is the product of the world it comes from: Victorian Britain. You will also need to be aware of what the examiners for your particular question are looking for. For GCSE, it appears that most questions are, at the time of writing this guide, "extract based" (**see p. 13 of this PDF of a mock exam issued by AQA here**); you will be given a small extract and asked to consider how the author builds suspense or drama in the extract, or presents the characters in a particular way. In order to achieve highly, you will need to answer the question carefully and not simply re-tell the extract; this is something that I have seen many good students do. The A Level questions on *Jane Eyre* are much more like the ones posed in the **essay question section** of this study guide. Sometimes, you might be asked to compare the novel with other literary texts, depending upon the nature of the task and/or exam board. For A Level, you need to be aware of other literary critics' views on the novel.

You should consider a few key questions:

For extract questions, consider how has the author **built up** to this particular moment. Think carefully about what the reader already knows before they have read the extract. You will need to know the story well in order to do this.

What literary devices does the author use to make the passage interesting or to reveal a particular character in a certain light? Think very carefully about the author's use of language: Brontë's use of descriptions to create a certain atmosphere or paint a sketch of a character/event; her use of dialogue to reveal character and create drama/tension; her use of imagery (metaphors/similes/personification). You will need to pack your essay full of the relevant terminology if you want to aim for higher marks as it appears many mark schemes as a key requirement.

You need to be aware of a number of different interpretations of the novel. The section on **Literary Criticism** should help you with this.

Finally, you need to provide evidence and analysis to back up your points. As a cornerstone of your essay writing technique, you should be aware of the **PEEL** method of analysing texts: making a Point, providing Evidence, Explaining how your evidence endorses your point, and Linking to a new point.

Useful links

(A word of warning: while the following websites are useful to look at, please do not copy them blindly. Read them carefully and make your own judgements. The highest marks are gained by students who have their **own** views.)

The Signet Classics' Teachers' Guide to Jane Eyre contains an excellent vocabulary list if you are struggling, good summaries and a useful character list. It's aimed at teachers, but students could easily use it and it's free:
http://www.penguin.com/static/pdf/teachersguides/JaneEyreT G.pdf
The Universal Teacher website although quite old now is very good:
http://www.universalteacher.org.uk/prose/janeeyre.htm
The Universal Teacher also has a good section on wide reading essays which might include *Jane Eyre*, scroll down to find the section which compares *Jane Eyre* with *Pride and Prejudice*:
http://www.universalteacher.org.uk/prose/wideread.htm
The Gradesaver website has a useful section on the typical questions on Jane Eyre, together with some explanation about how to answer the questions. While it is helpful to read their comments, you must remember to provide your own points and evidence as well:
http://www.gradesaver.com/jane-eyre/study-guide/essay-questions
SparkNotes has a similar website to Gradesaver's:
http://www.sparknotes.com/lit/janeeyre/study.html
The BBC Bitesize website covers many essential points and includes nice quizzes etc.:

http://www.bbc.co.uk/schools/gcsebitesize/english_literature/prosejaneeyre/

The Shmoop website has its familiar irreverent resources on *Jane Eyre* which are useful, particularly its section on literary devices:

http://www.shmoop.com/jane-eyre/literary-devices.html

The E-notes website has a detailed section on *Jane Eyre*:

http://www.enotes.com/topics/jane-eyre/in-depth

This website is good for finding quotes to illustrate literary devices:

http://selinaahwang1314520.blogspot.co.uk/2010/12/jane-eyre-literary-devices.html

Now have a go at one or more of the essay questions that follow.

Essay Questions on the Novel

Why do you think *Jane Eyre* was a bestseller when it was first published?

Why do some critics view *Jane Eyre* as a revolutionary text?

To what extent is *Jane Eyre* an allegory?

To what extent is *Jane Eyre* a Christian novel?

To what extent is *Jane Eyre* a story with a moral message?

To what degree is *Jane Eyre* a Gothic novel?

'*Jane Eyre* is a novel about the evils of oppression'. To what extent do you agree with this statement?

'*Jane Eyre* is a fairytale dressed up as a novel.' Discuss this statement, explaining why you agree or disagree with it.

To what extent is *Jane Eyre* a feminist novel?

To what extent is *Jane Eyre* ultimately a novel about colonial oppression?

Glossary

Authorial An adjective meaning 'belonging to the author or writer'

Autobiography A personal account of the author's own life, with the events usually relayed in the order in which they happened

Bluebeard A terrifying figure in a fairytale who locked up and killed his wives

Byronic Like Lord Byron; i.e. romantic, passionate, immoral, sexually promiscuous in some contexts

Contexts The worlds from which a text is created and emerges; the social, biographical and literary background to a text

Dynamic (n) Movement

Elliptical Concise, perhaps surprising

Genre Type of text, e.g. horror, sci-fi, Gothic

Gothic An adjective describing narratives which are full of supernatural happenings and extreme emotions, involving damsels in distress in haunted castles

Fundamentalism The idea that religious texts should be taken literally and obeyed absolutely, e.g. Christian fundamentalists insist that the story of Adam and Eve actually did happen.

Hero / heroine The main character (male / female) in a narrative, who exhibits truly fine qualities

Homophone A word which sounds the same as another but is spelt differently, e.g. 'there, their, they're'

Imagery All the poetic devices in a text, in particular the visual images created for the reader's mind to feed on and the comparisons that make a reader think and reflect upon an issue

Melodrama A story with extreme emotional events and characters, e.g. suicides, threats, blackmail, mad wives, lustful husbands

Novel A made-up, extended story

Protagonist The main character

Radical Extreme (politically or otherwise)

Realism In literature, a movement which aimed to simulate 'reality' in fiction

Satire – A work which mocks or ridicules (usually humorously) an individual or a prevailing trend (adj. satirical)

Sensibility / Sensibilities A characteristic of people who think deeply and responsively about issues

Subversive Troublesome, rebellious, seeking to overthrow a current system

Symbolic Representative of a particular issue or message, e.g. Bertha Mason's cutting of the bridal dress is symbolic of Rochester's betrayal of her

Theme An important idea in a text

Tone An atmosphere conveyed in the writing

Victorian Belonging to the UK's Victorian era (i.e. the reign of Queen Victoria, 1837–1901)

About the Author

Francis Gilbert is a Lecturer in Education at Goldsmiths, University of London teaching on the PGCE Secondary English programme and the MA in Children's Literature with Professor Michael Rosen. Previously, he worked for a quarter of a century in various English state schools teaching English and Media Studies to 11-18 year olds. He has also moonlighted as a journalist, novelist and social commentator both in the UK and international media. He is the author of 'Teacher On The Run', 'Yob Nation', 'Parent Power', 'Working The System -- How To Get The Very Best State Education for Your Child', and a novel about school, 'The Last Day Of Term'. His first book, 'I'm A Teacher, Get Me Out Of Here' was a big hit, becoming a bestseller and being serialised on Radio 4. In his role as an English teacher, he has taught many classic texts over the years and has developed a great many resources to assist readers with understanding, appreciating and responding to them both analytically and creatively. This led him to set up his own small publishing company FGI Publishing (fgipublishing.com) which has published his study guides as well as a number of books by other authors, including Roger Titcombe's 'Learning Matters'.

He is the co-founder, with Melissa Benn and Fiona Millar, of The Local Schools Network, **www.localschoolsnetwork.org.uk**, a blog that celebrates non-selective state schools, and also has his own website, **www.francisgilbert.co.uk** and a Mumsnet blog, **www.talesbehindtheclassroomdoor.co.uk**. He has appeared numerous times on radio and TV, including Newsnight, the Today Programme, Woman's Hour and the Russell Brand Show. In June 2015, he was awarded a PhD in Creative Writing and Education by the University of London.

Made in the USA
Monee, IL
01 September 2022

13078216R00038